BAPTISM

WHAT DO THE SCRIPTURES TEACH?

BAPTISM

WHAT DO THE SCRIPTURES TEACH?

TIMOTHY KLAVER

ISBN-10: 1981708545
ISBN-13: 978-1981708543

Dedicated to all who have been baptized into Christ Jesus, being united to and identified with Him.

CONTENTS

ACKNOWLEDGEMENTS

I would like to thank my God, my Lord and Saviour Christ Jesus, for having provided me the opportunity to write this book and get it into the hands of my brothers and sisters in Christ so that they, too, may be set free by knowing the truth, for "you shall know the truth, and the truth shall make you free" (John 8:32). This book is written with the purposes in mind to:

1. glorify God and honour His Son (Romans 15:6; Colossians 1:18), and
2. educate the body of Christ regarding truth (2 Timothy 2:15; 3:16; Acts 17:11; 1 Corinthians 2:13).

I would also like to thank you, the reader, for picking up this book. It is by no accident that you have. I pray that you have picked it up because you are interested in learning the truth about what the Bible has to say on this very important subject, and that you are willing to obey God's Word and conform yourself to the truths revealed therein. As you read, may God open your eyes so that you can see precisely what He has written in His Word and what He has not. It is for you that I have put this book together. May God bless it for that purpose.

Thank you, one and all.

INTRODUCTION:
CIRCUMSTANTIAL EVIDENCE

Books, movies, and television consistently attempt to downplay circumstantial evidence as if it is not enough to convict a criminal of a crime. This is *false*, and it is just one of *hundreds* of lies perpetuated in books, movies, and television that the average person is utterly ignorant to and gets brainwashed by because of *frequent repetition*. If you repeat a lie loud enough, long enough, and often enough, the average person will begin to believe it because of their sheer ignorance.[1] That is why public school systems exist, so that the government can dictate what our children learn and indoctrinate them all at once by brainwashing

---

[1] Ignorance does not in any way, shape, or form denote or connote stupidity. The literalness of a word is its denotation; the broader associations we have with a word are its connotations. "A person can be ignorant (not knowing some fact or idea) without being stupid (incapable of learning because of a basic mental deficiency). And those who say, 'That's an ignorant idea' when they mean 'stupid idea' are expressing their own ignorance." —Paul Brians, *Common Errors in English Usage* (Wilsonville, OR: William James & Co., 2009), 118.

them with false information. As I frequently state, education merely serves to teach you how to think and believe the way your teachers think and believe. Unless it is something like mathematics, it rarely ever teaches you how to think objectively, rationally, or logically, let alone how to think for yourself. Present day society does not like people who can think for themselves, whether in the work force or elsewhere. This is especially true of modern-day Liberals who want to silence the truth and other people's opinions, forcing people to accept opinions that are contrary to facts and evidence. This is demonstrated more and more on a frequent and consistent basis.

Circumstantial evidence is *indirect evidence*. Eye witnesses, including video footage, are *direct evidence*. Everything else is circumstantial evidence. A fingerprint at a crime scene is merely circumstantial evidence. The same weapon found at a person's house is circumstantial evidence. In many cases, circumstantial evidence is all that exists and is *more than enough* in convicting a criminal of a crime. Here are a few quotes taken from legal books with regard to circumstantial evidence:

Circumstantial Evidence
n. Evidence in a trial which is not directly from an eyewitness or participant and requires some reasoning to prove a fact. There is a public perception that such evidence is weak ("all they have is circumstantial evidence"), but the probable conclusion from the circumstances may be so strong that there can be little doubt as to a vital fact ("beyond a reasonable doubt" in a criminal case, and "a preponderance of the evidence" in a civil case). Particularly in criminal cases, "eyewitness" ("I saw Frankie shoot Johnny") type evidence is often lacking and may be unreliable, so circumstantial evidence becomes essential. Prior threats to the victim, fingerprints found at the scene of the crime, ownership of the murder weapon, and the accused being seen in the neighborhood, certainly point to the suspect as be-

ing the killer, but each bit of evidence is circumstantial.

Circumstantial Evidence in the law of evidence, indirect evidence of a fact in issue. An inference of the fact in issue can be made from a consideration of a number of other facts. It is sometimes spoken of as a chain but better considered as a cable: the more strands, the stronger, and the absence of one of the strands does not break the connection. The lay person often considers it in some way inferior, but not the lawyer, who appreciates the difficulties inherent in direct eyewitness evidence. Nonetheless, it is only as good as the strands that comprise it. These may have to be evaluated in their own right, otherwise a sound inference maybe based on a defective premise, as where Othello, asking for proof of Desdemona's infidelity, was answered by Iago: 'It is impossible you should see this, Were they as prime as goats, as hot as monkeys, As salt as wolves in pride, and fools as gross As ignorance made drunk: but yet I say, If imputation and strong circumstances, Which lead directly to the door of truth, Will give you satisfaction, you might have it.' (Act 3, Scene 3, line 400).

Circumstantial Evidence

Information and testimony presented by a party in a civil or criminal action that permit conclusions that indirectly establish the existence or nonexistence of a fact or event that the party seeks to prove.

Circumstantial Evidence is also known as indirect evidence. It is distinguished from direct evidence, which, if believed, proves the existence of a particular fact without any inference or presumption required. Circumstantial evidence relates to a series of facts other than the particular fact sought to be proved. The party offering circumstantial evidence argues that this series of facts, by reason and experience, is so closely associated with the fact to be proved that the fact to be proved may be inferred simply from the existence of the circumstantial evidence.

The following examples illustrate the difference between direct and circumstantial evidence: If John testifies that he saw Tom raise a gun and fire it at Ann and that Ann then fell to the ground, John's testimony is direct evidence that Tom shot Ann. If the jury believes John's testimony, then it must conclude that Tom did in fact shoot Ann. If, however, John testifies that he saw Tom and Ann go into another room and that he heard Tom say to Ann that he was going to shoot her, heard a shot, and saw Tom leave the room with a smoking gun, then John's testimony is circumstantial evidence from which it can be inferred that Tom shot Ann. The jury must determine whether John's testimony is credible.

Circumstantial evidence is most often employed in criminal trials. Many circumstances can create inferences about an accused's guilt in a criminal matter, including the accused's resistance to arrest; the presence of a motive or opportunity to commit the crime; the accused's presence at the time and place of the crime; any denials, evasions, or contradictions on the part of the accused; and the general conduct of the accused. In addition, much scientific evidence is circumstantial, because it requires a jury to make a connection between the circumstance and the fact in issue. For example, with fingerprint evidence, a jury must make a connection between this evidence that the accused handled some object tied to the crime and the commission of the crime itself.

Books, movies, and television often perpetuate the belief that circumstantial evidence may not be used to convict a criminal of a crime. But this view is incorrect. In many cases, circumstantial evidence is the only evidence linking an accused to a crime; direct evidence may simply not exist. As a result, the jury may have only circumstantial evidence to consider in determining whether to convict or acquit a person charged with a crime. In fact, the U.S. Supreme Court has stated that "circumstantial evidence is intrinsically no different from testimonial [direct] evidence" (Holland v. United States, 348 U.S. 121, 75 S. Ct. 127, 99 L. Ed. 150 [1954]). Thus, the distinction between direct and circumstantial evidence has little practical effect in the presentation or admissibility of evidence in trials.

> *West's Encyclopedia of American Law, edition 2.*
> *Copyright 2008 The Gale Group, Inc. All rights reserved.*

When addressing the circumstantial evidence surrounding the baptismal accounts in the Bible, each individual piece of circumstantial evidence must be looked at and catalogued in order to determine the proper mode of baptism. When studying the Bible, we need to look at *all* the evidence, both direct and indirect. Circumstantial evidence is frequently enough to decide a case, and that is precisely what we intend to do. We are going to examine the various baptisms in Scripture, as well as the key verse used as a proof text, in order to determine the truth and see what the Bible has to say about Baptism.

Lord God, I thank You immensely for those who have picked up a copy of this book, and I thank You that they have an interest in both biblical and spiritual things. This subject is often a very heated one, often with emotions running hot. I pray that You would grant each person reading this to have an open mind, to look at the circumstantial evidence, and to conform their beliefs according to the facts. Your Word is truth. You have the words of eternal life. Bless each individu-

al reading this book, and help them to study these things themselves and to come to a right understanding of Scripture, strengthening their faith in You. May You receive all the glory from this project, Lord, for Your name's sake. In Jesus' name, Amen.

Yours because of Calvary,
Timothy Klaver

"Not to us, O LORD, not to us, But to Thy name give glory." **–Psalm 115:1**

"Not in words taught by human wisdom, but in those taught by the Spirit." **–1 Cor. 2:13**

"Then He opened their minds to understand the Scriptures." **–Luke 24:45**

SECTION 1

1

ROMANS 6:3-4
EISEGESIS vs. EXEGESIS

Context is very important. It cannot be emphasized enough. Cults, and people with cult-oriented thinking, like to single out verses and take them at face value—*out of context*—while attempting to tie them together with other singled-out verses. This is one of the reasons I do not agree with the foolishness of having a favourite Bible verse (or even individual verse memorization), because 99 times out of 100 those verses are taken and used *entirely* out of context. Plus, those verses generally *do not* speak a single solitary thing to the individual other than what they "feel" it means or what they "think" it is saying. In other words, it is their current choice for favourite verse because of what *they* want it to say—*not* because of what it *actually* says or means.

Everyone who names the name of the Lord needs to be like the noble Bereans and study the Bible *thoroughly*, paying *extremely* close attention to what it is they are reading and *carefully* thinking about what they have read. If you get to a verse that pops out at you and your thinking tells you it is a good verse, ask yourself *why* it is a good verse. Ask yourself a number of questions about that verse: who, what, when, where, why, and how type questions. If you cannot remember a thing prior to that verse that can tell you what that verse means or how it relates to everything prior, then you *have not* been paying attention. You have merely glossed over the words as you read. This means you need to go back and start again. If you have to read a passage 10 times over, then do so. Better to have the correct understanding of a passage than for your understanding to epitomize this: Blah blah-blah blah important-for-some-reason blah blah blah-blah blah blah.

Sadly, yes, that is precisely how the majority of people read the Bible. More than likely because they open it and read it without the guidance of the Holy Spirit. The Bible is *not* like other books. You *cannot* simply open it and read and expect understanding to come. It is *spiritually* discerned. If you are not relying on the Spirit to help and guide you as you read, then most of what you read will be like looking through a foggy haze. The bits that stand out as clear will inevitably be out of context. People do this with Romans 6 through 8 all the time: "Chapter 6. Blah blah blah-blah blah blah. Chapter 7. Blah blah-blah blah blah... Ooh! My *experience* 'feels like' verses 14-25. Chapter 8. There is now no condemnation for those who are in Christ Jesus, blah blah blah-blah blah." The context has been completely done away with. Even though *everything* said in chapters 6 and 8 contradict the *assumed* meaning of 7:14-25, people still run with their feelings and experiences on this. What does all of this have to do with the passage at hand? It is meant to impress the importance of *context* upon you. With all that said, let us examine our passage.

> What shall we say then? Are we to continue in sin that grace might increase? May it never be! How shall we who died to sin still live in it? Or do you not know that all of us who have been baptized into

Christ Jesus have been baptized into His death? Therefore we have been buried with Him through baptism into death, in order that as Christ was raised from the dead through the glory of the Father, so we too might walk in newness of life. For if we have become united with Him in the likeness of His death, certainly we shall be also in the likeness of His resurrection, knowing this, that our old self was crucified with Him, that our body of sin might be done away with, that we should no longer be slaves to sin; for he who has died is freed from sin. (**Romans 6:1-7**)

Have you ever stopped to think about what this passage is saying? Have you ever stopped and asked yourself what this passage pertains to? When we read/study the Bible, we *cannot* simply take Scripture at face value, whether by the words the translators chose to use or by the divisions of chapters and verses (which never existed in the original manuscripts or copies). We must always start with 1:1 and examine the context before and after the current portion of Scripture we are reading/studying. There are three rules I strive to adhere to when I read/study the Bible:

1. *Context, context, context!* You need to consider the immediate (surrounding verses), sectional (surrounding chapters), and/or canonical (other passages) contexts, as well as the language, cultural, geographical, and historical gaps (or contexts).
2. *Compare Scripture with Scripture!* Even when expositing Scripture verse-by-verse, you need to consult the whole counsel of God's Word, otherwise isolating a passage to the book it is contained in can lead to some very bad interpretations.
3. *Wrestle with and submit to what the text actually says, and conform your beliefs accordingly.* When you

study Scripture openly and honestly, you are inevitably going to challenge some of your presently held beliefs. You need to be obedient to the Lord and conform your beliefs accordingly, regardless of your emotions. Anything less is disobedience, which is rebellion.

Let me ask you some questions. What were the circumstances of Jesus' burial? He was taken down from the cross and put in a new tomb by Joseph of Arimathea. What was the tomb like? Was is six-feet deep in the earth? No, it was not. It was carved out of rock. What do the Scriptures say about the burial? His body was carefully laid in the tomb, and a stone was rolled against the door (Mark 15:46). Was Jesus' body, when he was buried, *put down into the earth*, and when it was resurrected, did it *come up out of the earth*? Of course not! Jesus' burial was like taking someone, putting them in a closet, and closing the door. Robert Lewis Dabney had this to say:

By making baptism the commemoration of Christ's burial, and resurrection, the sacramental analogy (as well as the warrant) is totally lost. This analogy is not in the element to the grace; for in that aspect, there can be no resemblance. Water is not like a tomb, nor like the Holy Ghost, nor like Christ's atoning righteousness. Nor is bread like a man's body, nor wine like his blood. The selection of the sacramental element is not founded on a resemblance, but on an analogy. Distinguish. The bread and wine are elements, not because they are like a body and blood, in their qualities: but because there is a parallel in their uses, to nourish and cheer. So the water is an element of a sacrament, because there is a parallel in its uses, to the thing symbolized. The use of water is to cleanse. Where now is any analogy to Christ's burial? Nor is there even a resemblance

in the action, not even when the immersionist's
mode is granted. Water is not like a Hebrew tomb.
The temporary demission of a man into the former,
to be instantly raised out of it, is not like a burial.[2]

What would you think of a denomination that bases its fun-
damental position on a passage of Scripture written thirty or
forty years *after* Christ's ascension, when the writer had *no intention* to teach anything on the subject? Paul referred to baptism only *incidentally*, to illustrate a point that had *no bearing*
on his main subject *whatsoever*. We could search through the
four Gospels and Acts (or, for that matter, the entire Bible) and
not find any other references that imply anything like what the
Baptists suggest. In Romans 6:3-4, baptism is being used as an
illustration. But what is Paul actually illustrating? Let us examine the immediate context:

For while we were still helpless, at the right time
Christ died for the ungodly. For one will hardly die
for a righteous man; though perhaps for the good
man someone would dare even to die. But God
demonstrates His own love toward us, in that while
we were yet sinners, Christ died for us. Much more
then, having now been justified by His blood, we
shall be saved from the wrath of God through Him.
For if while we were enemies, we were reconciled to
God through the death of His Son, much more, having been reconciled, we shall be saved by His life.
And not only this, but we also exult in God through
our Lord Jesus Christ, through whom we have now
received the reconciliation. Therefore, just as
through one man sin entered into the world, and
death through sin, and so death spread to all men,
because all sinned—for until the Law sin was in the

---

[2] Robert Lewis Dabney, *Systematic Theology* (Carlisle, PA: Banner of
Truth, 2002), 760-761.

world; but sin is not imputed when there is no law. Nevertheless death reigned from Adam until Moses, even over those who had not sinned in the likeness of the offense of Adam, who is a type of Him who was to come. But the free gift is not like the transgression. For if by the transgression of the one the many died, much more did the grace of God and the gift by the grace of the one Man, Jesus Christ, abound to the many. And the gift is not like that which came through the one who sinned; for on the one hand the judgment arose from one transgression resulting in condemnation, but on the other hand the free gift arose from many transgressions resulting in justification. For if by the transgression of the one, death reigned through the one, much more those who receive the abundance of grace and of the gift of righteousness will reign in life through the One, Jesus Christ. So then as through one transgression there resulted condemnation to all men, even so through one act of righteousness there resulted justification of life to all men. For as through the one man's disobedience the many were made sinners, even so through the obedience of the One the many will be made righteous. And the Law came in that the transgression might increase; but where sin increased, grace abounded all the more, that, as sin reigned in death, even so grace might reign through righteousness to eternal life through Jesus Christ our Lord. (**Romans 5:6-21**)

Paul has been saying that where sin increases, grace abounds all the more. Some of his listeners might conclude that since grace is greatest where sin is strongest, we should let sin continue so that grace may abound. But Paul says, "May it never be! How shall we who died to sin still live in it?" *Then* he introduces his illustration in verse 3. If being "baptized into

Christ Jesus" means to be united with Christ, that is, to be "in Christ" (as it clearly does), then what do you suppose is meant by "baptized into His death"? Jesus is our *propitiation*, our *substitute*, so obviously Jesus' death becomes ours. Jesus is our representative. Jesus' death becomes our death through our union with Him. Colossians 2:12 bears out the same truth. How do we secure that union? Through baptism. Being "baptized into Christ Jesus." What kind of baptism? Water baptism? Of course not! How many people have been baptized by water who have never given their life to Christ?

Verse 4 uses the word "therefore," which means we should ask the question, "What is it there for?" The word "buried" is tied to the overall topic by the word "therefore," indicating that it results from something previously stated. "Buried with," translated from the Greek word *sunthapto* (συνθαπτω), literally means "buried *together* with." It is applicable *only* to burial in earth—*not* burial in water. *No one* would render it "to immerse." Burial with Christ refers to participating in His death by virtue of union with Him. Both burials (Jesus *and* His people) were one—they were buried together. How are we buried with Him? By "baptism into death." This *cannot* mean anything different than the previously-discovered fact from verse 3. Think of it this way: Jesus is a jar, we are a jellybean. If that jar is placed beneath a tree, where is the jellybean? In the jar, beneath the tree. If that jar is placed in a refrigerator, where is the jellybean? In the jar, in the refrigerator. If that jar is placed in a cupboard on a shelf, where is the jellybean? In the jar, in a cupboard on a shelf. Whatever happens to the jar happens to the jellybean.

When Jesus died, we died by virtue of our union with Him. When Jesus was buried, we were buried by virtue of our union with Him. When Jesus was resurrected, we were resurrected by virtue of our union with Him. When Jesus ascended into Heaven, we ascended into Heaven by virtue of our union with Him. When Jesus sat down on the throne, we sat down on the throne by virtue of our union with Him. Romans 6:3-4 is about *identi-*

fication—not water baptism.

Where is water mentioned in this passage? Where is there a reference to the *mode* of baptism in this passage? Based on what we have just discussed, *no one* can draw the ridiculous conclusion that water baptism itself is what unites us to Christ. It is the Holy Spirit that unites us to Christ. Baptists interpret this passage eisegetically, seeing in it what they want to get out of it, thereby imposing on the text something that simply *is not* there. If Jesus' burial had been exactly like a typical burial, would immersion be the proper way to symbolize it? Of course. But that is *not* how Jesus was buried, and baptism has *nothing* to do with His death, burial and resurrection. In fact, Jesus' burial had *nothing* to do with His work in saving sinners!

Let me ask you some more questions. What would have been different if, after dying at about the ninth hour, Jesus' body had been left on the cross until Sunday morning, and then He had come back to life and come down from the cross? Nothing! Is burial essential in order to prove His death? No. Is the essential part of His resurrection the point of His coming out of the tomb, or simply His coming back to life? Quite obviously His coming back to life, which He could have done even if He had not been buried. Ergo, Jesus' burial had *nothing* to do with His work in saving sinners. Observe a few words from Robert Lewis Dabney:

> If we may judge by the two sacraments of the old dispensation, and by the supper, sacraments (always few) are only adopted by God to be commemorative of the most cardinal transactions of redemption. Christ's burial was not such. Christ's burial is nowhere proposed to us as an essential object of faith. His death and the Spirit's work are. His death and resurrection are; the former already commemorated in the other sacrament. And besides; it would seem strange that the essential work of the Holy Ghost should be commemorated by no sacrament, while

that of Christ is commemorated by two! In the old dispensation the altar and the laver stood side by side. And here would be a two-fold covenant, with two seals to one of its promises, and none to the other![3]

If circumcision were still the rite of initiation into the church and signified our union with Christ, Romans 6:3-4 would read, *"Or do you not know that all of us who have been <u>circumcised</u> into Christ Jesus have been <u>circumcised</u> into His death? Therefore we have been buried with Him through <u>circumcision</u> into death, in order that as Christ was raised from the dead through the glory of the Father, so we too might walk in newness of life."* In similar fashion, Matthew Henry made this application in Romans 2:28-29: *"For he is not a <u>Christian</u> who is one outwardly; neither is <u>baptism</u> that which is outward in the flesh. But he is a <u>Christian</u> who is one inwardly; and <u>baptism</u> is that which is of the heart, by the Spirit, not by the letter; and his praise is not from men, but from God."* In these two passages, you can interchange the words and they teach the exact same truths. Both circumcision and baptism are signs and seals of the covenant of grace—one past, one present. Both circumcision and baptism are symbols of the Spirit's work. Both circumcision and baptism represent the cleansing of the heart.

For I do not want you to be unaware, brethren, that our fathers were all under the cloud, and all passed through the sea; and all were baptized into Moses in the cloud and in the sea; and all ate the same spiritual food; and all drank the same spiritual drink, for they were drinking from a spiritual rock which followed them; and the rock was Christ. Nevertheless, with most of them God was not well-pleased; for they were laid low in the wilderness. (**1 Corinthians 10:1-5**)

---

[3] *Ibid.* 761.

Is there anyone who, upon reading this passage, understands "baptized into Moses" as speaking of *actual* baptism, of *water* baptism? No? Good! So answer me this: Why do *so many* Christians, including Reformers and Puritans, falsely understand "baptized into Christ" and "baptized into His death" as speaking of *our* actual baptism, of *our* water baptism? Seriously! These men were good, godly Christians, men I can only aspire to be like, but come on! When they made interpretational errors of this magnitude, it is no wonder the modern church is making the same interpretational errors. Especially when men and women let traditions and experiences guide them rather than Scripture. What was the most notable thing about the Bereans? "They received the Word with great eagerness, examining the Scriptures daily, to see whether [the things that the Apostle Paul taught them] were so" (Acts 17:11). Scripture *must* be held higher than traditions, experiences, etc. Everything else *must* be subjected to and judged by Scripture.

In 1 Corinthians 10:2, baptism is being used to show identification. It is the exact same with Romans 6:3-4. There is no mode of baptism in view here. There is no water baptism in view here. It is an illustration used incidentally. Do you see now why *context* is so important? We either see a particular verse or set of verses in connection with the surrounding context with complete clarity, or we see a particular verse or set of verses in connection with the surrounding context with a foggy haze. The verse or set of verses by themselves are completely useless if we do not see the surrounding context with complete clarity. If the surrounding context is a foggy haze to us, then we can make that verse or set of verses say and mean pretty much whatever we want. We all know this is precisely what has been done with verses like John 3:16.

Take the Bible seriously. Read and study it with all seriousness, first praying and asking for the Holy Spirit's guidance before you open it. Be like the noble Bereans who checked to see if what the Apostle Paul was telling them was true or not. May God be with you all as you search and study His Word.

2

JESUS' BAPTISM

Then Jesus arrived from Galilee at the Jordan coming to John, to be baptized by him. But John tried to prevent Him, saying, "I have need to be baptized by You, and do You come to me?" But Jesus answering said to him, "Permit it at this time; for in this way it is fitting for us to fulfill all righteousness." Then he permitted Him. And after being baptized, Jesus went up immediately from the water; and behold, the heavens were opened, and he saw the Spirit of God descending as a dove, and coming upon Him, and behold, a voice out of the heavens, saying, "This is My beloved Son, in whom I am well-pleased." (**Matthew 3:13-17**)

What did Jesus mean when He said, "It is fitting for us to fulfill all righteousness" (v. 15)? *Righteousness* is a legal term. It differs from *holiness*. *Holiness* has to do with our inward purity, while *righteousness* involves our relationship to the law, whether we have done what the law requires or not. Jesus is our Great High Priest. In fact, He is the only *real* Priest who was ever in the world. Aaron's priesthood was only a representation of Christ's, so Aaron and his descendants may be called representative priests, and Christ called the real Priest. The Aaronic priesthood involved only the tribe of Levi, who were all descendants of Aaron. But look at what the writer of Hebrews says:

> For when the priesthood is changed, of necessity there takes place a change of law also. For the one concerning whom these things are spoken belongs to another tribe, from which no one has officiated at the altar. For it is evident that our Lord was descended from Judah, a tribe with reference to which Moses spoke nothing concerning priests. (**7:12-14**)

In verse 12, the author states, "For when the priesthood is changed, of necessity there takes place a change of law also." When the priesthood of Aaron was first instituted, the tribe was formally consecrated to be set apart for their high calling. Whether every priest from then on was set apart this way we do not know. But when a change took place as great as the one Hebrews speaks of, such as a change to *another tribe* (in connection with which, we are reminded, Moses said nothing about priests), then it would certainly be necessary for this new priest to comply with the law of consecration. It was this law that Jesus referred to when He said, "It is fitting for us to fulfill all righteousness." We find this law of consecration in Numbers 8:5-7.

> Again the LORD spoke to Moses, saying, "Take the Levites from among the sons of Israel and cleanse them. And thus you shall do to them, for their cleansing: <u>sprinkle</u> purifying water on them..."

How is it that Jesus was likely baptized? By immersion? That is assumed by sheer speculation. Let us examine the larger events of baptism in order to develop a right understanding. John the Baptist's ministry lasted about six months. We can estimate that he baptized a few hundred thousand people. That is an average of thousands of people per day! Could you imagine John standing waste deep in water for multiple hours a day, six days a week, for six months? What does water do to your hands and feet the longer you are in it? What kind of strength would John need to endure immersing people for multiple hours a day, six days a week, for six months? Are you starting to see the problem?

For argument's sake, let us say John only baptized 10,000 during his ministry. Let us say that during his ministry John only baptized for four days each week. In one hundred days, if he averaged 100 immersions per day, allowing three minutes per immersion, John would have had to stand in the water for five hours straight each day. What do you think the likelihood of that was? It is almost certain that no one could endure that kind of exertion for such a long time, let alone if he had been doing it to thousands of people per day. John's method of baptism would have no doubt been based on something from the Scriptures, some corresponding ceremony in the Old Testament. Hebrews 9:19 helps to provide the likely answer:

> For when every commandment had been spoken by Moses to all the people according to the Law, he took the blood of the calves and the goats, with water and scarlet wool and hyssop, and sprinkled both the book itself and all the people.

John most likely baptized using a hyssop branch. This branch was particularly well-suited, and often used, for that purpose. Using this method, John could have *easily* baptized thousands of people in a day without strenuous effort. Circumstantial evidence simply does not bode well for immersion.

These logical difficulties destroy the credibility of immersion.

When Scripture says "Jesus went up immediately from the water" (Matt. 3:16) or "And immediately coming up out of the water" (Mark 1:10), it simply means that He walked *out of* the water. People assume by their reading of Matthew and Mark that as soon as Jesus rose from His immersion that the Spirit descended upon Him. *Nowhere* does Scripture say Jesus went *under* the water. Luke's account helps us prove this by giving us further information: "Now it came about when all the people were baptized, that Jesus also was baptized, and while He was praying, heaven was opened, and the Holy Spirit descended upon Him in bodily form like a dove, and a voice came out of heaven, 'Thou art My beloved Son, in Thee I am well-pleased'" (v. 21-22). Furthermore, let us examine two Greek words that appear in the accounts of Matthew and Mark. The Greek word *anabaino* (αναβαινω) translated as "went up" and "coming up" means "to go up, ascend up, climb." The Greek word *apo* (απο) translated as "from" and "out of" can also be translated as "away from." In other words, both passages make complete sense when we understand they are speaking of Jesus *walking up onto* the shore *away from* the water, where He would then pray and the Holy Spirit descend upon Him: "Jesus *ascended* immediately *away from* the water" and "immediately *ascending away from* the water."

If we consider this information from an *a priori* standpoint, what we might expect or anticipate about things beforehand based on the nature of how they are, it will help us greatly in our understanding. The requirements in the Old Testament were often taxing, requiring great effort and self-denial on the part of the worshipers. The New Testament demands much simpler service, and the sacraments are easier to administer. Compare the Passover to the Lord's Supper. Also, compare circumcision to baptism.

Tell me what is wrong with these real-life examples (we have all read or heard of such cases). There are people who, in the dead of winter, will travel miles from the location of their church and chop holes in the ice just to be able to immerse people. There are other people who will travel dozens of miles from the location of their church just to be able to immerse people. Stories of immersions can get more and more complicated and require people to undergo more and more hardship to contend with the inconvenience. Where is the simplicity of worship in such actions? Anyone willing to perform this sacrament under such trying conditions deserves great credit, and this spirit of self-righteousness is one of the things that makes immersion appeal to people the way it does. Immersion is much closer by practice to the law of Moses, or even the Pharisees, than the simplicity of worship in the New Testament. The purpose of baptism is to *symbolize the gift of the Holy Spirit*. This process is best symbolized by the *application of water*.

There is one more consideration that we must take into account with regard to John's baptizing. John 3:23 says, "John also was baptizing in Aenon near Salim, because there were many streams there." *Aenon* is the plural of *fountain* or *spring*. Therefore, "many streams" is a more accurate translation than "much water," agreeing with the Greek text. If we were to go to Aenon today, we would find many springs trickling through marshy meadow on their way to the Jordan. Why would John leave an abundance of water at the Jordan (where he initially started baptizing) for a bunch of springs (that were not deep enough for immersion)? Simple. The Jordan was filthy. We know this from Naaman's words: "Are not Abanah and Pharpar, the rivers of Damascus, better than all the waters of Israel? Could I not wash in them and be clean?" (2 Kings 5:12). At this time of year, the Jordan was a foul, muddy flood that overflowed its banks (Josh. 3:15). John knew the insistent requirement of the law, that he should sprinkle them with clean water for baptism, so the cool clear water of the "many springs" at Aenon would be a more suitable location.

Based on the circumstantial evidence and logical difficulties, Jesus would have been baptized by John using a hyssop branch, dipped in the water and sprinkled over Him. The water descending upon Him symbolized the descending of the Spirit, which would soon transpire. Simplicity of worship. Not strenuous exertion.

After careful examination of all the circumstantial evidence, there is *no way* baptism by immersion can be exegeted from this passage.

3

THE BAPTISM OF THE 3,000

Now when they heard [Peter's sermon], they were pierced to the heart, and said to Peter and the rest of the apostles, "Brethren, what shall we do?" Peter said to them, "Repent, and each of you be baptized in the name of Jesus Christ for the forgiveness of your sins; and you will receive the gift of the Holy Spirit. For the promise is for you and your children and for all who are far off, as many as the Lord our God will call to Himself." And with many other words he solemnly testified and kept on exhorting them, saying, "Be saved from this perverse generation!" So then, those who had received his word were baptized; and that day there were added about three thousand souls.

They were continually devoting themselves to the apostles' teaching and to fellowship, to the breaking of bread and to prayer. Everyone kept feeling a sense of awe; and many wonders and signs were taking place through the apostles. And all those who had believed were together and had all things in common; and they began selling their property and possessions and were sharing them with all, as anyone might have need. Day by day continuing with one mind in the temple, and breaking bread from house to house, they were taking their meals together with gladness and sincerity of heart, praising God and having favor with all the people. And the Lord was adding to their number day by day those who were being saved. (**Acts 2:37-41**)

On the day of Pentecost, 3,000 people were baptized and added to the church. Peter's sermon started in the morning, around the third hour of the day (v. 15). We do not know how long it lasted. If the Apostles were given six hours with which to baptize 3,000 people, each of the twelve Apostles would have to perform 42 baptisms every hour. That is one immersion every 90 seconds! Even if you were to allow three minutes per each immersion, it would have taken 12 hours to baptize all 3,000 people. What do you think the likelihood of that was? Remember that the majority of the Jewish people and leaders were enemies of the Christians. There would have been at least two obstacles for them to overcome: (1) finding a place that could accommodate so many immersions; and (2) being allowed to perform them once this place had been found. Not to mention the preparation of the amount of water that they would require beforehand. It is quite evident that this sermon was spontaneous. So what do you think the likelihood is that any of the 3,000 people just happened to be wandering around with a change of clothes in case a baptism were to take place? Circumstantial evidence simply does not bode well for immersion in this situation either. These logical difficulties destroy the credibility of immersion.

After careful examination of all the circumstantial evidence, there is *no way* baptism by immersion can be exegeted from this passage.

4

THE ETHIOPIAN EUNUCH'S
BAPTISM

But an angel of the Lord spoke to Philip saying, "Arise and go south to the road that descends from Jerusalem to Gaza." This is a desert place. And he arose and went; and behold, there was an Ethiopian eunuch, a court official of Candace, queen of the Ethiopians, who was in charge of all her treasure; and he had come to Jerusalem to worship. And he was returning and sitting in his chariot, and was reading the prophet Isaiah. And the Spirit said to Philip, "Go up and join this chariot." And when Philip had run up, he heard him reading Isaiah the prophet, and said, "Do you understand what you are reading?" And he said, "Well, how could I, unless someone guides me?" And he invited Philip to come up and sit with him. Now the passage of Scripture which he was reading was this: "HE WAS LED AS A SHEEP TO SLAUGHTER; AND AS A LAMB

BEFORE ITS SHEARER IS SILENT, SO HE DOES NOT OPEN HIS MOUTH. IN HUMILIATION HIS JUDGMENT WAS TAKEN AWAY; WHO SHALL RELATE HIS GENERATION? FOR HIS LIFE IS REMOVED FROM THE EARTH." And the eunuch answered Philip and said, "Please [tell me,] of whom does the prophet say this? Of himself, or of someone else?" And Philip opened his mouth, and beginning from this Scripture he preached Jesus to him. And as they went along the road they came to some water; and the eunuch said, "Look! Water! What prevents me from being baptized?" And Philip said, "If you believe with all your heart, you may." And he answered and said, "I believe that Jesus Christ is the Son of God." And he ordered the chariot to stop; and they both went down into the water, Philip as well as the eunuch; and he baptized him. And when they came up out of the water, the Spirit of the Lord snatched Philip away; and the eunuch saw him no more, but went on his way rejoicing. But Philip found himself at Azotus; and as he passed through he kept preaching the gospel to all the cities, until he came to Caesarea. (**Acts 8:26-40**)

Let us examine the circumstantial evidence pertaining to this passage and see if we can determine the truth regarding the Ethiopian eunuch's baptism. If we study geography, we know that Gaza was roughly forty or fifty miles southwest of Jerusalem. Scripture informs us that this was "a desert place" (v. 26). If we were to go to this location today, we would find that it is still a desert place, where the only water is that of the occasional spring trickling down from the hillside and forming small pools before being absorbed by the sand. Stories in the Old Testament inform us that this was a poorly watered area where wells had to be dug just to provide water for animals. There are accounts in the story of Abraham of such wells (Gen. 21:25-31), and

Abraham's servant who went to find Isaac a wife stopped at just such a well where Rebekah came out to fetch some water (Gen. 24:10-21). From Genesis 26:12-22, Exodus 2:16-22, and other passages, we learn that these wells were valuable property in that region. These logical facts concerning the quality of the land do not point to a good chance of finding enough water for immersion.

By the Ethiopian eunuch exclaiming, "Look! Water!," and asking, "What prevents me from being baptized?," he must have known something about baptism already. He was reading from the middle of Isaiah 53, which we learn from the quote in Acts 8:32-33. He must have been studying it for quite some time. Remember, chapters and verses did not exist in the Scriptures at that time. If we examine the context of the passage in Isaiah 53, is there anything nearby that could have suggested the subject of baptism to him?

> Thus He will <u>sprinkle</u> many nations, Kings will shut their mouths on account of Him; For what had not been told them they will see, And what they had not heard they will understand. (**Is. 52:15**)

When Philip and the eunuch came to water, no doubt the passage he had read earlier was still fresh on his mind, thus prompting him to ask, "What prevents me from being baptized?" The Greek text shows the Eunuch's surprise at finding water. No doubt Philip would have explained the importance of the *Spirit's work* and how the water in baptism is merely a *symbol* of the Spirit's cleansing, which is poured upon or sprinkled on those who trust in Jesus as their Lord and Saviour.

When it says they "went down into the water" and they "came up out of the water," all this means is that they walked into the water and walked out of the water. If I walk from the shore to the middle of a creek or stream that only comes to my ankles, I have "went down into the water." When I walk from the middle of the creek or stream back onto the shore, I have "came up out of the water." The Greek word *katabaino* (καταβαινω) translated as "went down" simply means "to descend." The Greek word *anabaino* (αναβαινω) translated as "came up" simply means "to ascend." The Greek word *eis* (εις) translated "into" is where we get our term *eisegesis* from, referring to the reading *into* of a text ideas and concepts that simply are not there. The Greek word *ek* (εκ) translated "out of" simply means "from." Immersion is *not* in view here, otherwise Philip got baptized as well.

What is the likelihood that after an immersion baptism, Philip travelled 20 miles to Azotus dripping wet? There is no mention of preparation in this passage, such as dry clothing (or having a change of clothes), or any other passage related to baptism. If one's hypothesis concerning this account is that the Ethiopian eunuch was immersed, all the probabilities of circumstantial evidence point against it. Sprinkling or pouring are the more likely means by which the Ethiopian eunuch was baptized.

After careful examination of all the circumstantial evidence, there is *no way* baptism by immersion can be exegeted from this passage.

5

PAUL'S BAPTISM

Now Saul, still breathing threats and murder against the disciples of the Lord, went to the high priest, and asked for letters from him to the synagogues at Damascus, so that if he found any belonging to the Way, both men and women, he might bring them bound to Jerusalem. And it came about that as he journeyed, he was approaching Damascus, and suddenly a light from heaven flashed around him; and he fell to the ground, and heard a voice saying to him, "Saul, Saul, why are you persecuting Me?" And he said, "Who art Thou, Lord?" And He [said,] "I am Jesus whom you are persecuting, but rise, and enter the city, and it shall be told you what you must do." And the men who traveled with him stood speechless, hearing the voice, but seeing no one. And Saul got up from the ground, and though his eyes were open, he could see nothing; and leading him by the hand, they brought him into Damascus. And he was three days without sight, and neither ate nor drank.

Now there was a certain disciple at Damascus, named Ananias; and the Lord said to him in a vision, "Ananias." And he said, "Behold, here am I, Lord." And the Lord said to him, "Arise and go to the street called Straight, and inquire at the house of Judas for a man from Tarsus named Saul, for behold, he is praying, and he has seen in a vision a man named Ananias come in and lay his hands on him, so that he might regain his sight." But Ananias answered, "Lord, I have heard from many about this man, how much harm he did to Thy saints at Jerusalem; and here he has authority from the chief priests to bind all who call upon Thy name." But the Lord said to him, "Go, for he is a chosen instrument of Mine, to bear My name before the Gentiles and kings and the sons of Israel; for I will show him how much he must suffer for My name's sake." And Ananias departed and entered the house, and after laying his hands on him said, "Brother Saul, the Lord Jesus, who appeared to you on the road by which you were coming, has sent me so that you may regain your sight, and be filled with the Holy Spirit." And immediately there fell from his eyes something like scales, and he regained his sight, and he arose and was baptized; and he took food and was strengthened. Now for several days he was with the disciples who were at Damascus, and immediately he began to proclaim Jesus in the synagogues, saying, "He is the Son of God." And all those hearing him continued to be amazed, and were saying, "Is this not he who in Jerusalem destroyed those who called on this name, and who had come here for the purpose of bringing them bound before the chief priests?" But

Saul kept increasing in strength and confounding the Jews who lived at Damascus by proving that this Jesus is the Christ. (**Acts 9:1-22**)

Let us examine the circumstantial evidence pertaining to this passage and see if we can determine the truth regarding Paul's baptism. Verse 9 of this chapter says that Paul "was three days without sight, and neither ate nor drank." Obviously his physical condition would have been weak. According to verse 19, what happened? "And he took food and was strengthened." If Paul was in great physical weakness, and you were planning to immerse him, when would the best time for doing so be? Clearly, as soon as he regained his strength. Would you have immediately went to look for a place to immerse him, or would you have first given him a morsel of food in order to strengthen him? According to Scripture, when did Paul's baptism take place relative to when he ate?

And immediately there fell from his eyes something like scales, and he regained his sight, and he arose and was baptized; and he took food and was strengthened. (**v. 18-19**)

If one reads this passage in the original Greek, the circumstantial evidence mounted against the assumed speculation of immersion becomes even more clear. In *every* account, we find Ananias saying, "Get up and be baptized" (22:12-16), or the statement, "he got up and was baptized" (9:17-18). This can be literally translated as: "rising up, he was baptized," or, "standing up, he was baptized." How could Paul have possibly been baptized by immersion if he was baptized immediately where he stood when he rose to his feet? The circumstantial evidence in this passage is especially in favour of sprinkling or pouring.

After careful examination of all the circumstantial evidence, there is *no way* baptism by immersion can be exegeted from this passage.

Baptism

6

THE PHILIPPIAN JAILER'S BAPTISM

And it happened that as we were going to the place of prayer, a certain slave-girl having a spirit of divination met us, who was bringing her masters much profit by fortunetelling. Following after Paul and us, she kept crying out, saying, "These men are bond-servants of the Most High God, who are proclaiming to you the way of salvation." And she continued doing this for many days. But Paul was greatly annoyed, and turned and said to the spirit, "I command you in the name of Jesus Christ to come out of her!" And it came out at that very moment. But when her masters saw that their hope of profit was gone, they seized Paul and Silas and dragged them into the market place before the authorities, and when they had brought them to the chief magistrates, they said, "These men are throwing our city into confusion, being Jews, and are proclaiming customs which it is not lawful for us to accept or to observe, being Romans." And the crowd rose up together against them, and the chief magistrates tore their robes off them, and proceeded to order them to be beaten with rods. And when they had inflicted many blows upon them, they threw them into prison, commanding the jailer to guard them securely; and he, having received such a command, threw them into the inner prison, and fastened their feet in the stocks.

But about midnight Paul and Silas were praying and singing hymns of praise to God, and the prisoners were listening to them; and suddenly there came a great earthquake, so that the foundations of the prison house were shaken; and immediately all the doors were opened, and everyone's chains were unfastened. And when the jailer had been roused out of sleep and had seen the prison doors opened, he drew his sword and was about to kill himself, supposing that the prisoners had escaped. But Paul cried out with a loud voice, saying, "Do yourself no harm, for we are all here!" And he called for lights and rushed in and, trembling with fear, he fell down before Paul and Silas, and after he brought them out, he said, "Sirs, what must I do to be saved?" And they said, "Believe in the Lord Jesus, and you shall be saved, you and your household." And they spoke the word of the Lord to him together with all who were in his house. And he took them that very hour of the night and washed their wounds, and immediately he was baptized, he and all his household. And he brought them into his house and set food before them, and rejoiced greatly, having believed in God with his whole household.

Now when day came, the chief magistrates sent their policemen, saying, "Release those men." And the jailer reported these words to Paul, saying, "The chief magistrates have sent to release you. Now

2off2

therefore, come out and go in peace." But Paul said to them, "They have beaten us in public without trial, men who are Romans, and have thrown us into prison; and now are they sending us away secretly? No indeed! But let them come themselves and bring us out." And the policemen reported these words to the chief magistrates. And they were afraid when they heard that they were Romans, and they came and appealed to them, and when they had brought them out, they kept begging them to leave the city. And they went out of the prison and entered the house of Lydia, and when they saw the brethren, they encouraged them and departed. (**Acts 16:16-40**)

Let us examine the circumstantial evidence pertaining to this passage and see if we can determine the truth regarding the Philippian jailer's baptism. Paul and Silas were thrown in jail because God, through them, removed a spirit of divination from a young woman, thereby costing her masters their means of profit. After having been beaten, they were thrown in prison and the magistrates commanded the head jailer to "guard them securely" (v. 23). How did the jailer carry out this order? By "[throwing] them into the inner prison, and fasten[ing] their feet in the stocks" (v. 24). What can we determine from verse 24 concerning the layout of the prison? Clearly there was an outer section—likely with cells for ordinary prisoners, and an inner section—likely for holding certain prisoners more securely.

The Bible tells us that around midnight there was an earthquake that shook all the doors of the prison open. When the jailer awoke and saw that all the prison doors were opened, he assumed that all the prisoners had escaped. He was about to kill himself when Paul shouted at him, assuring him that all the prisoners were still present. What does the Bible say that the jailer did next? "He called for lights and rushed in and, trembling with fear, he fell down before Paul and Silas, and after he brought them out, he said, 'Sirs, what must I do to be saved?'"

(vv. 29-30). What did the jailer bring Paul and Silas out of? Where did he bring them into? They were in the inner prison, so quite obviously the jailer brought them out of there and into the outer section of the prison.

After Paul and Silas answered the jailer's question and told him what he must do to be saved, what did he do? "He took them that very hour of the night and washed their wounds" (v. 33a). Then what happened? "Immediately he was baptized, he and all his household" (v. 33b). Wait! His entire household was baptized? How is this possible? Where was his household? Did Paul and Silas leave the prison in the middle of the night to go to his house and baptize him and his entire family? Verses 32-35 are the most troubling of this passage. Verse 32 informs us that Paul and Silas "spoke the word of the Lord to him together with all who were *in his house.*" Verse 33 informs us that "he and *all his household*" were baptized. Verse 34 informs us that "he brought them *into his house* and set food before them, and rejoiced greatly, having believed in God with his whole household." The most likely answer to these questions is that the jailer had his own quarters in the prison. He was the commanding jailer, after all. I am not sure how many places are still like this today, but when I was younger, and in the past, it was not unreasonable or unheard of for the owner or property manager to have their own quarters on the grounds. Churches, hotels, apartment buildings, universities, etc. This is where we need to understand *historical context* and not try to see the passage through our eyes and experiences.

Is it likely that the jailer's baptism was done by immersion? Do you think it would have happened in the prison? Do you think there would be sufficient water inside a prison for an immersion baptism? Have you *ever* heard of *any* prison having such facilities? The means for prisoners to be able to drown other prisoners? I did not think so. There *was* a river near Philippi. Is it possible they went there to baptize the jailer? So, the jailer locked up all the other prisoners, took his entire household, went with Paul and Silas down to the river at approximately two o'clock in the morning to be baptized, all were fully immersed, and then they returned to the prison so the jailer could prepare a meal for the two disciples? Why not simply wait until daylight? What was the rush? Especially considering churches today will wait months, even years, before applying "believer's" baptism. Do you see the logical difficulties here with the concept of baptism by immersion? But that is not all.

In the morning, the magistrates told the jailer to release Paul and Silas. What was their response? "But Paul said to them, 'They have beaten us in public without trial, men who are Romans, and have thrown us into prison; and now are they sending us away secretly? No indeed! But let them come themselves and bring us out.'" (v. 37). Why would Paul and Silas refuse to leave the prison until the magistrates came and released them publicly, if they had already been outside the prison during the middle of the night *without* the permission of the magistrates? Add one more logical difficulty to the pile.

Here is yet another logical difficulty that must be overcome: Paul and Silas had been lashed not many hours earlier. Do you not think that baptism by immersion would be quite the task for two men in their beaten condition at such a late hour in the night?

After careful examination of all the circumstantial evidence, there is *no way* baptism by immersion can be exegeted from this passage.

Baptism

7

BAPTISM:
HOW SHOULD IT BE ADMINISTERED

Jesus' burial had *nothing* to do with His work in saving sinners! No doubt this statement offends many, but let us examine the truth of it. As we asked before, what would have been different if, after dying at about the ninth hour, Jesus' body had been left on the cross until Sunday morning, and then He had come back to life and come down from the cross? Nothing. Is burial essential to prove His death? No. Is the essential part of His resurrection the point of His coming out of the tomb, or simply coming back to life? Clearly, coming back to life, which he could have done even if He had not been buried. Ergo, Jesus' burial had *nothing* to do with His work in saving sinners. There is nothing worth commemorating there.

The Lord's Supper commemorates the death of Jesus. We see the brokenness of His body in the breaking of the bread, and we see the shedding of His blood in the drinking of the wine. The Lord's resurrection is commemorated every Sunday when we gather together for worship. So what does baptism commemorate?

Baptism was not meant to symbolize or commemorate burial. It was intended to symbolize the receiving of and the work of the Spirit. By examining this symbolism, it will help to shed some light on the *mode* of baptism. If the Bible had said, "Christ will be buried in the earth, but you shall be buried by baptism in the water," that would settle the issue of immersion. Nobody could explain away a statement like that. So what do we do with this statement, "I baptized you with water; but He will baptize you with the Holy Spirit" (Mark 1:8)? The great work of the Spirit is to cleanse, purify, and sanctify. Using water in baptism commemorates or symbolizes the work of the Spirit. The Bible frequently states that we are cleansed by Christ's blood, too. "For there are three that bear witness, the Spirit and the water and the blood; and the three are in agreement" (1 John 5:8). The Bible teaches us that all three—the Holy Spirit, the water, and the blood—cleanse and purify us. While this verse is contested as to whether or not it belongs in the text, nevertheless it agrees with the whole of Scripture on this point.

The Holy Spirit plays an integral part in our salvation. He convicts us of sin, draws us to turn to Jesus, regenerates and sanctifies us. If the Lord's Supper refers exclusively to the work of Christ, then baptism refers exclusively to the work of the Holy Spirit. Let us look at some passages dealing with the work of the Spirit:

"Until the Spirit is *poured out upon* us from on high." **Isaiah 32:15a**

"For I will *pour out* water on the thirsty land And streams on the dry ground; I will *pour out* My Spirit on your offspring, And My blessing on your descendants." **Isaiah 44:3**

"And I will not hide My face from them any longer,

for I shall have *poured out* My Spirit on the house of Israel," declares the Lord GOD." **Ezekiel 39:29**

"And it will come about after this That I will *pour out* My Spirit on all mankind; And your sons and daughters will prophesy, Your old men will dream dreams, Your young men will see visions. And even on the male and female servants I will *pour out* My Spirit in those days." **Joel 2:28-29**

"And I did not recognize Him, but He who sent me to baptize in water said to me, 'He upon whom you see the Spirit *descending* and remaining upon Him, this is the one who *baptizes in the Holy Spirit.*'" **John 1:33**

"And immediately coming up out of the water, He saw the heavens opening, and the Spirit like a dove *descending* upon Him." **Mark 1:10**

"By the washing of regeneration and renewing by the Holy Spirit, whom He *poured out* upon us richly through Jesus Christ our Savior." **Titus 3:5c-6**

"Therefore having been exalted to the right hand of God, and having received from the Father the promise of the Holy Spirit, He has *poured forth* this which you both see and hear." **Acts 2:33** (Keep in mind the passage from Joel quoted in Acts 2:17-21.)

The words used to describe the work of the Holy Spirit are *baptized with*, *poured upon*, *poured out*, and *descending on*. Are there any passages that represent the work of the Holy Spirit as being anything like immersion? Some might attempt to refer to Acts 2:2, trying violently to force the word "filled" to somehow refer to being "enveloped" or "buried": "And suddenly there came from heaven a noise like a violent, rushing wind, and it filled the whole house where they were sitting." Note that this passage says nothing about the Spirit Himself, but that the *sound* filled the entire room. Not until the third verse do we see a manifestation of the Spirit's baptism. When it comes to baptism, is the individual *put into* the element, or is the element *applied* to him/her?

Baptism is meant to commemorate or symbolize the work of the Holy Spirit. What light does the work of the Holy Spirit throw on the question of the *mode* of baptism? Romans 6 is the *only* place where immersion *seems* to be taking place, and yet we have proven that that is *not* the case. Based on the use of the Greek words, we see pouring in Acts 1:5, Acts 11:15-16, and Acts 2:17; we see dipping (or partial immersion) in Matthew 26:23 and John 13:26; we see complete identification in 1 Corinthians 10:1-4; and we see sprinkling when we compare Hebrews 9:9-10 with Numbers 19:4, 13, 17-30, and then look at Hebrews 9:13-14. But where do we see complete immersion? The commitment to just one mode is not necessary based on the historical use of the words, but the work of the Spirit *clearly* indicates a pouring or sprinkling. Shower (pouring or sprinkling), bath (immersion).

Consider finally John 2:6: "Now there were six stone waterpots set there for the Jewish custom of purification, containing twenty or thirty gallons each." Jews could not possibly have immersed themselves in one of these jars, let alone their tables or couches (see Mark 7:4). Immersion in Scripture is purely speculation. Second Timothy 2:15 applied like a Berean will exegetically eliminate all concepts of immersion imposed on the texts (including those of Jesus going to the Jordan to be baptized by John). There is *no* biblical grounds for baptism by immersion.

When you study this subject out for yourself, use only the Bible as your authoritative source and do so in three stages:

1. Find the meanings of the words used based on their

contexts (*baptizo*, βαπτιζω; *baptisma*, βαπτισμα; *baptismos*, βαπτισμος; *baptistes*, βαπτιστης; *bapto*, βαπτω).

2. Study the significance of the ceremony, looking at what baptism was meant to symbolize or commemorate.
3. Carefully look at examples of baptism in the New Testament in order to discern the mode used.

Be completely honest with yourself and the results. Then be obedient to Christ and conform your beliefs to the findings.

Baptism

8

BAPTISM:
QUICK AND BIBLICAL

Too many churches today practice what they call "believer's baptism." I am sorry, but, biblically speaking, there is *no such thing*! It is biblical to baptize *very quickly*. On the day of Pentecost, 3,000 people were baptized moments after they heard Peter's Gospel sermon preached (Acts 2:41). The family of the Philippian jailer who heard the name of Jesus for the first time shortly after midnight, were all baptized by dawn (Acts 16:25-35). It is important to note that in the Greek, the belief is singular while the baptism is plural; the jailer believed and his entire family was baptized (including any children). The Ethiopian Eunuch heard the Gospel and then minutes (at most, hours) later was baptized in ditch water by the side of the road (Acts 8:36-38). After hearing the word of the Lord from Ananias, Paul got baptized before breaking an absolute fast that he had observed for three days (Acts 9:9, 18-19).

Those who claim we should exercise caution as to whom we should baptize have *no* Scriptures to support them. Simon

Magus was baptized in Acts 8:13, though he quickly proved how unworthy he was when he tried to buy the ability to give away the Holy Spirit. Peter essentially told him to go to Hell (Acts 8:20). Likewise, Demas, who had been a fellow-labourer of Paul's, proved how unworthy he was when he left Paul for the things of this world (2 Timothy 4:10).

The reason people believe we should exercise caution when baptizing is because they *do not* understand the meaning and purpose of baptism. If they practiced baptism the way we see it done in the Bible, not only would they understand this, but they would also understand infant baptism (which we will address in the next section). Except for the outward practice, *everything* about circumcision and baptism is *exactly* the same: Both are initiatory rites (Gen. 17:10-11; Matt. 28:19; Acts 2:38-39; 8:12-13); both signify an inward reality (Rom. 2:28-29; Col. 2:2-12; Phil. 3:3); both picture the death of the old man of sin (Rom. 6:3-7; Col. 2:11-12); both represent repentance (Jer. 4:4; 9:25; Lev. 26:40-41; Acts 2:38); both represent regeneration (Rom. 2:28-29; Titus 3:5); both represent justification by faith (Rom. 4:11-12; Col. 2:11-14); both represent a cleansed heart (Deut. 10:16; 30:6; Isa. 52:1; Acts 22:16; Titus 3:5-7); both represent union and communion with God (Gen. 17:7; Ex. 19:5-6; Deut. 7:6; Heb. 8:10); both indicate citizenship in Israel (Gen. 17:4; Gal. 3:26-29; Eph. 2:12-13; 4:5); both indicate separation from the world (Ex. 12:48; 2 Cor. 6:14-18; Eph. 2:12); and both can lead to either blessings or curses (Rom. 2:25; 1 Cor. 10:1-12; 11:28-30). Baptism replaced circumcision as the sign and seal of the covenant of grace. This fact is seen in Colossians 2:11-12 where Paul refers to "circumcision of Christ" as "baptism": "In [Jesus] you were also circumcised . . . having been buried with Him in baptism..."

You see, a person's baptism acts as a testimony *for* or *against* them, just as circumcision did. In the cases of Simon Magus and Demas, their baptism was a testimony against them that they were covenant breakers. If a church does not want to baptize infants, that is their choice, but *do not* claim that such a practice is not biblical based on your own ignorance and subjective opinion. "We must confess that some bring their children for this sacrament because of the sweetness of the ceremony, or because of the traditions of family and church, or even with the misguided expectation that somehow 'holy water' will magically protect their child from hell. Yet neither sentiment nor tradition nor superstition is sufficient reason for believers to bring their children to be baptized. And, thankfully, such reasons are not the basis of our church's practice. We baptize infants because we believe that the Bible teaches us to do so."[4]

What these churches should be doing when they baptize quick and biblical, is warning the people about the seriousness of the commitment they are making. Even Jesus warned potential disciples that following Him was a life-changing (even life-sacrificing) decision, telling them to count the cost of their decision. He said, "If anyone wishes to come after Me, let him deny himself, and take up his cross daily, and follow Me" (Luke 9:23). Frequently, Jesus' strong words seemed determined to drive people away who were less than wholehearted in their decision to follow Him and obey His commands (Luke 9:57-62; John 6:53-66). When we evangelize, we should be doing no less. We *should not* be watering down the Gospel and presenting an easy-believism in order to gain numbers.

Baptismal candidates should be baptized quickly, but *not* without first being warned of the seriousness of sealing forever their decision to follow Christ.

---

[4] Bryan Chapell, *Why Do We Baptize Infants?*, (Phillipsburg, NJ: P&R Publishing, 2006), p.1

Baptism

9

BAPTIST IN THE OLD TESTAMENT

In the Septuagint, the Greek translation of the Hebrew Scriptures, the Greek word *baptizo* (βαπτιζω) occurs very infrequently. Only twice, to be exact. In Isaiah 21:4, we read: "My heart goes astray and lawlessness baptizes my soul." The writer was changed from a state of quiet trust in God to fearfulness as a result of seeing great wickedness and knowing that terrible judgments would follow. The use of the word here implies a change (which we can also see from some of the New Testament usages).

"Of all the texts that might be cited from antiquity the one that gives greatest clarity to this issue is a text from a Greek poet and physician, Nicander, who lived about 200 B.C. In a recipe for making pickles he used both words. Nicander said that the vegetable should first be dipped (*baptō*) in boiling water and then baptized (*baptizō*) in the vinegar solution. ...

We could say the baptizing had identified the vegetable with the brine."[5]

Similarly, Galatians 3:27 says, "For as many of you as were baptized into Christ have put on Christ." In other words, the Christians in Galatia had been identified with Christ Jesus. We see the same thing in 1 Corinthians 10:1-2: "I want you to know, brethren, that our fathers were all under the cloud, and all passed through the seas, and all were baptized into Moses in the cloud and in the sea." This passage is especially significant in understanding baptism, since the people of Israel were obviously *not* "immersed" (the Baptist's favourite word for baptism) either in the sea or the cloud.

Let us look at the favourite verse on baptism that some cults twist out of context and draw false conclusions from: "He who believes and is baptized will be saved" (Mark 16:16). This verse has *never* meant that unless a person is baptized (immersed) in water, he/she cannot be saved. We know this conclusion is *wrong* because of the rest of Scripture. We are saved *by grace* through faith in the work of Christ on Calvary. This verse, like all verses dealing with baptism, is addressing the believer's identification and union with Christ.

The only other word found in the Septuagint is the Greek word *bapto* (βαπτω), occurring 18 times. They are as follows:

Exodus 12:22	dip hyssop in blood
Leviticus 4:6, 17	dip finger in blood
Leviticus 9:9	dip finger in blood
Leviticus 11:32	dip in water
Leviticus 14:6, 16, 51	dip in blood, in oil, in running water
Numbers 19:18	dip hyssop in water
Deuteronomy 33:24	dip foot in oil

[5] James Montgomery Boice, *Foundations of the Christian Faith*, (Downers Grove, IL: IVP Academic, 1986), 598.

Joshua 3:15	dipped in edge of water
Ruth 2:14	dip bread in vinegar
1 Samuel 14:27	dip staff in honey comb
2 Kings 8:15	dip in water
Job 9:31	dip into pit (plunge)
Psalm 68:23	dip in blood
Daniel 4:33	wet with the dew of heaven
Daniel 5:21	wet with the dew of heaven

With the *possible* exception of three of these passages, *none* of them can be used to support the concept of "immersion." This concept is derived eisegetically from the Baptist's misinterpretation of Romans 6:3-4 due to their failure to pay attention to the context of the passage. The majority of the above passages *all* speak of dipping something into something (without "immersion"), and some continue on to speak of sprinkling.

Baptism in the Bible more frequently than not is used figuratively or metaphorically to speak of a change of identity having taken place. When you examine 600 years of classical Greek literature (from about 400 B.C. to about 200 A.D.), you find that there is *no* definite translation for the words *bapto* and *baptizo*. If they meant "immersion" definitively, then our Bibles would have translated the words as "immersion." The fact that these words are transliterated rather than translated is demonstrative of the fact they *do not* have a definitive translation, as seen by Isaiah 21:4's translation of the Hebrew word *ba'ath* (בעת), which means "terrify, startle, fall upon": to input fear.

Baptism

10

MORE BAPTIST EISEGESIS

When reading Scripture, Baptists latch onto phrases like "went up immediately from the water" (Matt. 3:16), "immediately coming up out of the water" (Mark 1:10), "there was much water there" (John 3:23), "they both went down into the water" (Acts 8:38), and "they came up out of the water" (Acts 8:39), and read into them what they want them to say. This is known as *eisegesis*.

First of all, let us examine two Greek words that appear in the accounts of Matthew and Mark. The Greek word *anabaino* (αναβαινω) translated as "went up" and "coming up" means "to go up, ascend up, climb." The Greek word *apo* (απο) translated as "from" and "out of" can also be translated as "away from." In other words, both passages make complete sense when we understand they are speaking of Jesus *walking up onto* the shore *away from* the water, where He would then pray and the Holy Spirit would descend upon Him: "Jesus *ascended* immediately *away from* the water" and "immediately *ascending away from* the water." "Up out of the water" in no way indicates that Jesus had been submerged under the water.

Jay E. Adams mistakenly says, "In Mark's account *ek* is used, but in Matthew, *apo*." According to Jay P. Green's *The Interlinear Bible*, *The Englishman's Greek Concordance of the New Testament*, the Greek text found in *The English Hexapla*, the Greek text of the *Textus Receptus*, and the symbols and marginal notes of *The Newberry Bible*, *ek* (εκ) does not appear in Mark until verse 11. *Apo* (απο) is used in verse 10. Only according to the Greek text of the Nestle-Aland *Novum Testamentum Graece* is the word *ek* used. *Ek* appears in four (4) manuscripts (Sinaiticus, Vaticanus, Bezae, and Regius) while *apo* appears in all the others. Wayne Grudem erroneously argues, "The Greek text specifies that he came 'out of' (*ek*) the water, not that he came away from it (this would be expressed by Gk. *apo*)." Mr. Grudem is being deceitful with those words because even in the Nestle-Aland *Novum Testamentum Graece* in Matthew's account, the word *apo* is used, which Mr. Grudem acknowledges means "away from." Further, he should know very well that *ek* can be translated as "from" or even "away from," but *apo* cannot be translated as "out of."

Mark 1:11 – there came a voice *from* heaven
Mark 6:14 – the Baptist was risen *from* the dead
Mark 6:16 – he is risen *from* the dead
Mark 7:31 – departing *from* the coasts of Tyre
Mark 9:9 – were risen *from* the dead
Mark 9:10 – rising *from* the dead should mean
Mark 10:20 – these have I observed *from* my youth
Mark 10:37 – one *on* thy right hand, and the other *on* they left
Mark 10:40 – to sit *on* my right hand an don my left
Mark 11:8 – cut down branches *off* the trees
Mark 11:20 – fig tree dried up *from* the roots
Mark 11:30 – *from* heaven, or *of* men?
Mark 12:25 – when they shall rise *from* the dead

Mark 12:30 – thou shalt love the Lord thy God *with* all thy heart, and *with* all thy soul, and *with* all thy mind, and *with* all thy strength

Mark 12:33 – And to love him *with* all the heart, and *with* all the understanding, and *with* all the soul, and *with* all the strength

Mark 12:36 – Sit thou *on* my right hand

Mark 13:27 – his elect *from* the four winds

Mark 13:25 – I will drink no more *of* the fruit

Mark 15:27 – one *on* his right hand, and the other *on*

Mark 16:3 – roll us away the stone *from* the door

Mark 16:19 – sat *on* the right hand of God

Second of all, as we addressed earlier, John 3:23 says, "John also was baptizing in Aenon near Salim, because there were many streams there." *Aenon* is the plural of *fountain* or *spring*. Therefore, "many streams" is a more accurate translation than "much water," agreeing with the Greek text. If we were to go to Aenon today, we would find many springs trickling through marshy meadow on their way to the Jordan. Why would John leave an abundance of water at the Jordan for a bunch of springs? Simple. The Jordan was filthy. We know this from Naaman's words: "Are not Abanah and Pharpar, the rivers of Damascus, better than all the waters of Israel? Could I not wash in them and be clean?" (2 Kings 5:12). At this time of year, the Jordan was a foul, muddy flood that overflowed its banks (Josh. 3:15). John knew the insistent requirement of the law, that he should sprinkle them with clean water for baptism, so the cool clear water of the "many springs" at Aenon would be a more suitable location. Wayne Grudem is correct in stating, "it would not take 'much water' to baptize people by sprinkling, but it would take much water to baptize by immersion." However, Mr. Grudem makes assumptions here and then draws conclusions based on those assumptions. In his *Christian Theology*, Millard Erickson says, "immersionism seems the most adequate of the several positions," but as we have just discovered, there was *not* "much water" there; there were "many streams."

Augustus Hopkins Strong makes some blind and fallacious assertions in his *Systematic Theology* regarding baptism, which are based solely on his assumptions, conclusions drawn on assumptions, and eisegesis. He states that baptism is "immersion, and immersion only," claiming that the "command to baptize is a command to immerse." He claims he can show this from:

1. The usage of Greek writers—including the church Fathers, when they do not speak of the Christian rite, and the authors of the Greek version of the Old Testament.
2. Every passage where the word occurs in the New Testament either requires or allows the meaning 'immerse.'

Wayne Grudem likewise makes the same blind and fallacious assertions in his *Systematic Theology*: "The practice of baptism in the New Testament was carried out in one way: the person being baptized was immersed or put completely under the water and then brought back up again. Baptism by immersion is therefore the 'mode' of baptism or the way in which baptism was carried out in the New Testament."

First, the works of James W. Dale[6] regarding the historical usage of *baptizo* (βαπτιζω) utterly obliterate Mr. Strong's (and Mr. Grudem's) ridiculous assertions. Even the *Theological Dictionary of the New Testament* does not back Mr. Strong's position. Furthermore, 600 years of secular Greek history using a word in a particular way has *no bearing whatsoever* on how the writers of the New Testament used a word. Sometimes they would use a word completely different from how the rest of secular society used it. It is used throughout

---

[6] *Christic Baptism*; *Classic Baptism*; *Judaic Baptism*; *Johannic Baptism*; *Patristic Baptism*.

secular Greek history in numerous and varied ways. If
βαπτιζω meant "to immerse," then the word would have been
translated as "immerse" in our English Bibles and John would
have been known as John the Immersionist or John the Im-
merser. The fact is, βαπτιζω has been *transliterated*, and *not
translated*, because there exists *no* specific word with which
to translate this term accurately.

> "In the English Bible *baptizō* has generally been
> transliterated to give us the word *baptize*. When a
> word is transliterated into English from another lan-
> guage, it is quite often an indication of a multiplicity
> of meanings. Thus, if the word *baptizō* had lent itself
> to easy translation, an obvious English word would
> have been used to translate it. If *baptizō* had meant
> only "immerse," then *immerse* would be the word
> used. We would speak of "John the Immerser." Or
> we would recite, "Go therefore and make disciples
> of all nations, immersing them in the name of the
> Father and of the Son and of the Holy Spirit." "[7]

Second, Mr. Strong demonstrates his blind assertions
based on assumptions and conclusions drawn on assumptions
when he fallaciously states that "every passage where the
word occurs in the New Testament either requires or allows
the meaning 'immerse'." Mr. Strong has obviously failed to
pay attention to the details of each account of baptism presented in the New Testament, as well as failing to observe the
circumstantial evidence surrounding each case. When these
are examined, one quickly realizes that there is no room made
available for immersion. Not to mention that the practice of
immersion is more in line with the rigorous rituals required
under the Old Covenant than with the simplicity and ease of
service instituted under the New Covenant. Furthermore,
when you examine several of the passages mentioning bap-

---

[7] Boice, *Foundations of the Christian Faith*, 598.

tism, it quickly becomes apparent that they have *nothing* to do with water baptism whatsoever, but rather have to do with *identification*.

Mr. Strong makes many other false assertions with regard to baptism—its meaning, mode, and subjects, but I will only address one final absurd assertion of his. He claims that the "proper subjects of baptism are those only who give credible evidence that they have been regenerated by the Holy Spirit,—or, in other words, have entered by faith into the communion of Christ's death and resurrection." Not only does Mr. Strong eisegetically misapply Romans 6:3-4 here, but once again he fails to pay attention to the witness of the holy Scriptures. "To the law and to the testimony." Baptism identifies us with Christ, whether that identification is true or false. Baptism acts as a witness or testimony either for or against us. In the New Testament, whenever someone made a profession of faith, regardless whether that faith was genuine or not, they were *immediately* baptized. It was not withheld until they gave "credible evidence that they [had] been regenerated by the Holy Spirit." So Mr. Strong's assertion of giving "credible evidence" is destroyed by the very Scriptures themselves. Judas, Simon Magus, and Demas were all false converts, yet they made professions of faith and were all baptized. They identified themselves with Christ but were never united with Him.

While immersion might seem plausible with John's baptizing, being they were at the Jordan river with plenty of water, every other case of baptism renders immersion *impossible* by the details and facts. If we were holding a court case, based on the evidence, the Baptist's position for immersion would be weighed and found wanting. The case would be open and shut *against* immersion. The Baptist's strongest "proof text," Romans 6:3-4, *does not* even speak of water baptism, let alone mode of baptism.

SECTION 2

11

THE LAW AND BAPTISM

Once a law is put in place, how binding is it? How long does its authority last? A law is binding from the time it is passed until its obligation is satisfied, or until it is repealed. Jesus said, "Do not think that I came to abolish the Law or the Prophets; I did not come to abolish, but to fulfill. For truly I say to you, until heaven and earth pass away, not the smallest letter or stroke shall pass away from the Law, until all is accomplished." (Matt. 5:17-18). What he means by this is that the law will not be repealed or voided, or become no longer binding, in the smallest degree. The law will only be finished when all its commands are carried out and completed. Once the reason that a law was laid down has been fulfilled, it is no longer necessary to follow that law.

God said further to Abraham, "Now as for you, you shall keep My covenant, you and your descendants after you throughout their generations. This is My covenant, which you shall keep, between Me and you and your descendants after you: <u>every male among you shall be circumcised</u>. . . . and it shall be the sign of the covenant between Me and you." (Gen. 17:9-11)

Here is a law decreed and set forth by God Himself. It is both a *positive command* and a *the LORD God said*! How long did this law apply? Did it only apply to Israel?

Therefore, be sure that it is those who are of faith who are sons of Abraham. (Gal. 3:7)

And if you belong to Christ, then you are Abraham's offspring, heirs according to promise. (Gal. 3:29)

The covenant God made with Abraham was part of the covenant of grace: Abraham and his descendants would be saved by faith. The above passages clearly show who the descendants of Abraham are. A law is binding until it is either fulfilled or repealed. Show, from Scripture, that the command—the law requiring circumcision—is no longer binding. God requires the seal of the covenant to be made to the children in Abraham's line, which is now anyone who is in Christ, the heirs of the promise.

What I am saying is this: the Law, which came four hundred and thirty years later, does not invalidate a covenant previously ratified by God, so as to nullify the promise. For if the inheritance is based on law, it is no longer based on a promise; but God has granted it to Abraham by means of a promise. (Gal. 3:17-18)

Where, in Scripture, is there a *the LORD God said* that fulfills or repeals this command? Any laws from the Old Testament that have not been fulfilled or repealed are still binding. Most of the ceremonial laws foreshadowed Christ and His work and were indeed fulfilled by Him. Therefore, it is true that they have ended. The law that requires us to observe the Sabbath did not relate to Christ or His work, and was not fulfilled by Him. Therefore it is still binding. However, we see in Scripture that the specific day was substituted in order for us to commemorate the resurrection of Christ. The law requiring Abraham and his seed after him to apply the seal of the covenant to their infant children was also not related to Christ or His work, and was not fulfilled by Christ. Circumcision was ended through the very same process that caused Passover to end—what we call *substitution*.

The law that we are looking at has two important aspects to consider: First, and most importantly, it required parents to consecrate their children to God by applying the seal of the covenant to them; Second, at the time it was given, the law specified that this seal should be circumcision. The essential part of the law was the consecration itself—the applying of the seal. The rite, which was originally circumcision, could end if it were replaced with another rite, either of the *same kind* or for the *same purpose*. But the law itself, requiring children to be consecrated to God, stands to this day *unfulfilled* and *unrepealed*.

Baptism has replaced circumcision as the seal of the covenant. The two rites have the same purpose and the same significance. Both are initiatory rites into the church and both symbolize the purity of the heart. The law requiring children to be consecrated to God *has not been repealed*. The rite has merely been changed—from circumcision to baptism. The New Testament rite is simpler, but its purpose and significance are the same. The one takes the place of the other. Once, circumcision was the seal of the covenant; now, by the authority of God, it is baptism.

But if some of the branches were broken off, and

you, being a wild olive, were grafted in among them and became partaker with them of the rich root of the olive tree, do not be arrogant toward the branches; but if you are arrogant, remember that it is not you who supports the root, but the root supports you. You will say then, "Branches were broken off so that I might be grafted in." Quite right, they were broken off for their unbelief, but you stand by your faith. Do not be conceited, but fear; for if God did not spare the natural branches, neither will He spare you. (Rom. 11:17-21)

The tree is and has always been Christ. He is the *true* Israel. Jewish children grew up *in* this tree. Do the children of Gentiles who were grafted into this tree somehow grow up *separately* from this tree only to be grafted in later? Of course not! They now grow up *in* this tree, too. The same warnings that applied to the Jewish children also apply to them. All the apostasy passages in the New Testament are warnings to those who grow up in this tree to not neglect so great a salvation by becoming covenant breakers and wearing the sign and seal of the covenant hypocritically, which would only serve to increase their condemnation. Which means they would have been better off having never heard of Christ than to be a covenant breaker.

The sacrament of baptism is a beautiful thing commemorating the gift and work of the Holy Spirit. As Bryan Chapell has said, "We must confess that some bring their children for this sacrament because of the sweetness of the ceremony, or because of the traditions of family and church, o even with the misguided expectation that somehow 'holy water' will magically protect their child from hell. Yet neither sentiment nor tradition nor superstition is sufficient reason for believers to bring their children to be baptized. And, thankfully, such reasons are not the basis of our church's practice. We baptize infants because we believe that the Bible teaches us to do so."

Those who oppose infant baptism, performed correctly and biblically, are *taking from* the Word of God based on mere assumption. Let us be biblical Christians and administer this holy sacrament biblically.

Baptism

12

BAPTISM'S MEANING

The problem with understanding the purpose of baptism aris-es when Christians understand it to be a sign of faith, or a sign that one has received forgiveness of sins. When this is what we understand by baptism, then our understanding fails miserably. This problem is not averted by waiting until peo-ple make professions at an age of maturity, as has been demonstrated horrifically in our churches. We have seen far too many people baptized who do not have faith and/or whose lives clearly demonstrate that they are unregenerate. Further, by waiting until an age of maturity, we are being dis-obedient and are not following the biblical example. If we examine the book of Acts, any time someone made a profes-sion of faith, they were baptized immediately there on the spot. There was no waiting. If they were heads of their household, their entire household was baptized with them. Baptism was not a sign of their having come to faith, for we see several examples of those whose profession was false, such as Simon Magus (Acts 8:9-24) and Demas (2 Tim. 4:10). If baptism was a sign of one's faith, and is for believer's only, then it makes no sense at all why Scripture would contain warnings against apostasy (Heb. 10:28-30).

Baptism, like circumcision, is a sign and seal of the truth of God's promise—to give righteousness to all who have faith—and testifies in one of two ways: (1) it testifies to a blessing (that righteousness is given to those of faith); (2) it testifies to a curse (that those who break the covenant will be cut off). As with circumcision, baptism acts as a testimony or witness *for* or *against* an individual. Whether they received the sign and seal when they were a child or as an adult makes no difference. If they reject the faith, the sign and seal acts as a witness or testimony *against* them (consider Ishmael and Esau), that they are covenant breakers. If they embrace the faith, the sign and seal act as a witness or testimony *for* them (consider Isaac and Jacob), that they are covenant keepers.

Baptism and circumcision are different externally, but they are exactly identical internally. They represent the same things: both are initiatory rites (Gen. 17:10-11; Matt. 28:19; Acts 2:38-39; 8:12-13); both signify an inward reality (Rom. 2:28-29; Col. 2:2-12; Phil. 3:3); both picture the death of the old man of sin (Rom. 6:3-7; Col. 2:11-12); both represent repentance (Jer. 4:4; 9:25; Lev. 26:40-41; Acts 2:38); both represent regeneration (Rom. 2:28-29; Titus 3:5); both represent justification by faith (Rom. 4:11-12; Col. 2:11-14); both represent a cleansed heart (Deut. 10:16; 30:6; Isa. 52:1; Acts 22:16; Titus 3:5-7); both represent union and communion with God (Gen. 17:7; Ex. 19:5-6; Deut. 7:6; Heb. 8:10); both indicate citizenship in Israel (Gen. 17:4; Gal. 3:26-29; Eph. 2:12-13; 4:5); both indicate separation from the world (Ex. 12:48; 2 Cor. 6:14-18; Eph. 2:12); and both can lead to either blessings or curses (Rom. 2:25; 1 Cor. 10:1-12; 11:28-30).

Matthew Henry, commenting on Romans 2:28-29, wrote: "He is not a Christian that is one outwardly, nor is that baptism which is outward in the flesh; but is one inwardly, and baptism is that of the heart, in the spirit, and not in the letter, whose praise is not of men but of God." Baptism, whether by sprinkling, pouring, or dunking, is merely an outward demonstration of one's being dedicated to God for His purposes and uses. Yes, Scripture supports sprinkling, pouring, or dunking as baptism. Study the individual words out (*baptizo*, βαπτιζω; *baptisma*, βαπτισμα; *baptismos*, βαπτισμος; *baptistes*, βαπτιστης; *bapto*, βαπτω) and their usages and interpretations. How can you baptize a couch or table (Mark 7:4)? Baptism *does not* save, *does not* regenerate, and *does not* mean the individual truly belongs to, or will belong to, the Lord. Baptism *is not* a public declaration of one's faith, as we have proven with Simon Magus and Demas, and we have witnessed rampantly throughout the North American churches.

When you were born, were you born as a full citizen of your country with all the rights and responsibilities thereof? Yes, you were. However, because you were young, you did not know of these rights and responsibilities and could not appropriate them. You had to be taught them. When you were older, you then either embraced them as your own or rejected them, which is treason and demands you leave your country. The same is true concerning circumcision and baptism. The son circumcised on the 8th day had no faith of his own. He knew nothing of the covenant promises and had to be taught them. As he grew, he could then embrace what he was taught and appropriate the blessings unto himself, or reject what he was taught and appropriate the curses unto himself. Every time he looked at his circumcision it would be a reminder to him of what it testified.

The fact that *no* command was *ever* given in Scripture revoking the inclusion of children in the covenant is proof positive that infants of believing parents should be baptized. The several examples of household baptisms in the New Testament are also proof positive that infants of believing parents should be baptized. When you study the Greek construction behind these, you will find that one believed (singularly) but the entire household was baptized (plurally), which logically would have included children. It says nothing of their personal faith. If there was a change in the sign of the covenant and children were no longer included in that covenant, the Jews would have been *furious* because their children were now *worse off* than they were before. It would be quite understandable as to why. That is why Peter said, "The promise is for you and your children and for all who are far off, as many as the Lord our God will call to Himself" (Acts 2:39).

Those who come to this subject openly, honestly desiring to seek the truth of Scripture and know what it teaches so that they can conform their lives to it, will convert and embrace this doctrine wholeheartedly. God rewards those who diligently seek Him and reveals His truths to those who earnestly and honestly want to know them. Why do you suppose that so many credo-baptists are becoming paedo-baptists? What credible reason can you give as to their abandoning of credo-baptism other than the fact they studied the Scriptures and Scripture convinced them of paedo-baptism? Clearly their pre-supposition was toward credo-baptism, and all their arguments against paedo-baptism demonstrate the utter disdain they had for it. So what changed?

What does the historical record show? In his book *Infant Baptism Scriptural and Reasonable*, Samuel Miller consults church history. He quotes several church fathers from the third century who speak on the issue of infant baptism. He even refers to a discourse between Augustine and Pelagius. Pelagius denied that children are born with a sinful nature. So Augustine argued with him that if that is the case, then there is no need to baptize infants. Pelagius agreed to infant baptism and said he knew of no one who denied such a practice. Now, if infant baptism is unbiblical and was not taught by the Apostles, then *somewhere* in the 200-some years between their deaths and these church fathers of the third century, infant baptism *somehow* miraculously and mysteriously became the predominant practice without *anyone* noticing. One minute they were not practicing it and *POOF* the next minute they were, without *anybody* noticing the slightest change. How stupid do these people think we are?!? The first group of people to question infant baptism were an offshoot of the Waldenses, under a man named Peter de Bruis, referred to as Petrobrussians, 1200 years after Christ. The next group of people to question infant baptism were the Anabaptists 1500 years after Christ. Then later the Baptists under the erroneous interpretations of Dispensationalism and its dividing of Scripture, creating disunity between the Testaments by separating them and creating a "God of the Old Testament" and a "God of the New Testament" when there is only but *one* God of the *whole* Bible—*in unity*! So, for over 1600 years (excluding the Catholic perversion of the practice), until the Baptists came along, the *entire* Christian church was in unity over the teaching, practice, and defence of infant baptism.

Do yourself a favour, Christian, and be like the noble Bereans and *search* the Scriptures. Put off your traditions, put off your pre-suppositions, put off your personal feelings and opinions, and be like the noble Bereans and *search* the Scriptures. Seek God's truths with joy and a desire to conform your life to those truths. When those truths confront and challenge your current beliefs, submit yourself to them and conform yourself to them. This is the best advice I can give you.

Baptism

13

WHY DO PEOPLE DISAGREE WITH INFANT BAPTISM?

Several arguments arise when it comes to asking why certain individuals disagree with the practice of infant baptism. We will examine some of those arguments and answer them accordingly.

1. **They believe that the new covenant is made strictly between God and regenerate people only.**
   But if this were true, why does the new covenant repeatedly warn against apostasy? Hebrews 10:28-30, for example. There is absolutely no sense warning about apostasy if the new covenant is only between God and regenerate people because we know for a fact that, if you are a genuine convert, it is *impossible* for you to lose your salvation. Apostasy is committed by those who claim to have belonged to or believed in that faith and have since rejected it. The genuine

convert can do no such thing. Ergo, such warnings would be senseless, useless, and worthless.

2. **They believe that the new covenant is a brand new covenant that replaces the old covenant.**

   In truth, the word for "new" *does not* mean "brand new" but rather "fresh" or "renewed." Therefore, the new covenant is a renewed covenant that expands the former covenant—the covenant of grace. Some try and quote Hebrews 8:13 here, but the context of chapter 9 rebukes them. Anything that was a type or shadow and found its fulfillment in Christ is obsolete. Basically, the ceremonial aspects of the Mosaic Covenant. No one would contend that the Noahic Covenant is now obsolete, because we still have God's sign and seal of that covenant to this very day. Otherwise, He could flood the world again. Likewise, you could not contend that the Abrahamic Covenant (Gen. 17:7) is obsolete because Peter contends for it in Acts 2:39 ("The promise is for you and your children and for all who are far off, as many as the Lord our God will call to Himself") and Paul contends for it in Galatians 3 ("If you belong to Christ, then you are Abraham's descendants, heirs according to promise") and Ephesians 2 ("You were...strangers to the covenants of promise . . . you are no longer strangers"). The new covenant is a further expansion and final revelation of the covenant of grace that was first made with Adam.

3. **They believe that there is no explicit warrant (an example or a command) *for* infant baptism.**

   Likewise, there is no explicit warrant (an example or a command) *against* infant baptism. On this point, *both* are arguing from silence. Further, there is no explicit warrant (an example or a command) to exclude children from baptism, which would be required if God changed His dealings with His people. Therefore, the burden of proof rests with those who are against it. For over 2,000 years the Jews practiced the rite of the sign, seal, and pledge of circumcision with regard to the promise of the covenant of grace. Had this changed, there would be express command, by word or sample, in the Scriptures. The Jews would have objected to such a thing because their children would have been in a worse condition under the Gospel than they had been under the Law, which would have strengthened their prejudices against it. For everyone in their household to be included *except* for their children would have outraged them. Really, there is explicit warrant for the inclusion of children in the new covenant (Deut. 30:6; Jer. 31:36-37), in the church (Eph. 1:1 with 6:1-4; Col. 1:2 with 3:20; 1 Cor. 7:14), and in the kingdom (Matt. 19:14; Mark 10:14; Luke 18:16).

4. **They believe there are no examples of infant baptism in the Scriptures.**

   Likewise, there are no examples of believer's children later believing and being baptized. Again, *both* arguments from silence. You would think that considering the book of Acts spans like 40 years you would have such examples, but you do not. They are no better off for explicit verses to teach their practice. However, the examples of household baptisms *do* support the inclusion of children. It would be incredulous to believe that *none* of the members of these households had *any* children whatsoever (considering households consisted of spouse, children, slaves, and any relatives living with you). It would be even more incredulous (but not necessarily impossible) to state that *every* single one of them expressed faith. What we see is the heads of these households believing and their entire households being baptized. The household baptisms also demonstrate that God still deals with people according to households and headship representation. Adam was our head and represented us all when he sinned. Abraham was head and represented his entire household (children, slaves, relatives). Korah's entire household perished because of his rebellion. The man who stole silver brought his entire household under judgment and they were all stoned. The two sons that brought strange fire to the altar caused their father's house to be judged. David's house was judged because of his sin with Bathsheba. Individualism and its selfishness did not exist until the Renaissance. The entire globe, and many cultures *still* today, operated under the familial unit. We *cannot* take our mindset and way of life and impose it on the Scriptures!

5. **They believe that such a practice intimates that the child is a born-again believer.**

   If that were the case, then the practice of circumcision to the 8-day-old infant meant that he had expressed faith like Abraham (Rom. 4; Gal. 3) and was himself a believer. Any argument against infant baptism is necessarily an argument against infant circumcision. The sign and seal of circumcision and baptism does *nothing* for the individual's salvation. It merely sets them apart for God's use. The condition to be met of the covenant in the Old Testament as well as the New Testament is, has been, and always will be *faith*. When that condition is met, then the blessings that accompany the covenant belong to that individual. When that condition is not met, then the curses that accompany the covenant belong to that individual. Only the heresy of the Roman Catholic Church attests that baptism saves and regenerates. This is why the warnings of apostasy under the new covenant exist; because that child may be set apart for God by his parents, but reject God entirely. *Eve-*

rything that belongs to the believer is set apart for God's use, and God wants to redeem *everything* connected to the believer. The creation never sinned, yet it waits to be redeemed. Why? From what? It gets redeemed in connection to man's redemption. God has always wanted to redeem man, man's household, and man's society. Case in point, Noah is said to have been the *only* righteous man on the earth, and yet God redeemed his family with him.

6. **They believe that baptism and circumcision are completely different from each other in every way.** The truth is, only the external practice of each is different. The internal representation of each is exactly the same. Both are initiatory rites (Gen. 17:10-11; Matt. 28:19; Acts 2:38-39; 8:12-13); both signify an inward reality (Rom. 2:28-29; Col. 2:2-12; Phil. 3:3); both picture the death of the old man of sin (Rom. 6:3-7; Col. 2:11-12); both represent repentance (Jer. 4:4; 9:25; Lev. 26:40-41; Acts 2:38); both represent regeneration (Rom. 2:28-29; Titus 3:5); both represent justification by faith (Rom. 4:11-12; Col. 2:11-14); both represent a cleansed heart (Deut. 10:16; 30:6; Isa. 52:1; Acts 22:16; Titus 3:5-7); both represent union and communion with God (Gen. 17:7; Ex. 19:5-6; Deut. 7:6; Heb. 8:10); both indicate citizenship in Israel (Gen. 17:4; Gal. 3:26-29; Eph. 2:12-13; 4:5); both indicate separation from the world (Ex. 12:48; 2 Cor. 6:14-18; Eph. 2:12); and both can lead to either blessings or curses (Rom. 2:25; 1 Cor. 10:1-12; 11:28-30). Baptism replaced circumcision as the sign and seal of the covenant of grace. This fact is seen in Colossians 2:11-12 where Paul refers to "circumcision of Christ" as "baptism": "In [Jesus] you were also circumcised . . . having been buried with Him in baptism..." Again, "baptism" here has *nothing* to do with water baptism. It is about *identification*,

unity.

7. **They believe that infant baptism is not biblical and was not taught by the Apostles.**

In his book *Infant Baptism Scriptural and Reasonable*, Samuel Miller consults church history. He quotes several church fathers from the third century who speak on the issue of infant baptism. He even refers to a discourse between Augustine and Pelagius. Pelagius denied that children are born with a sinful nature. So Augustine argued with him that if that is the case, then there is no need to baptize infants. Pelagius agreed to infant baptism and said he knew of no one who denied such a practice. Now, if infant baptism is unbiblical and was not taught by the Apostles, then *somewhere* in the 200-some years between their deaths and these church fathers of the third century, infant baptism *somehow* miraculously and mysteriously became the predominant practice without *anyone* noticing. One minute they were not practicing it and *POOF* the next minute they were, without *anybody* noticing the slightest change. How stupid do these people think we are?!? The first group of people to question infant baptism were an offshoot of the Waldenses, under a man named Peter de Bruis, referred to as Petrobrussians, 1200 years after Christ. The next group of people to question infant baptism were the Anabaptists 1500 years after Christ. Then later the Baptists under the erroneous interpretations of Dispensationalism and its dividing of Scripture, creating disunity between the Testaments by separating them and creating a "God of the Old Testament" and a "God of the New Testament" when there is only but *one* God of the *whole* Bible—*in unity*! So, for over 1600 years (excluding the Catholic perversion of the practice), until the Baptists came along, the *entire* Christian church was in unity over the teaching, practice, and defense of infant baptism.

I was raised with the Baptist view of baptism. After looking thoroughly at Scripture and church history, I have become convinced that infant baptism is right, proper, and biblical. Some people have it done out of tradition, some have it done out of the beauty of the ceremony, and some have it done out of erroneous misconceptions and superstitions that it will somehow magically protect their child from Hell. *None* of these reasons is sufficient for believers to baptize their children. We do so because God commands it and wants to be a God to us and to our children.

Those who disagree with and deny infant baptism do so *apart* from the Scriptures. They do so based on their presuppositions, their traditions, and their personal feelings. *All* of Scripture and church history stands *against* them. They disagree with and deny it out of *rebellion* and *disobedience*. By doing so, they count their *own precious children* to be among the pagans, where even Scripture made a difference between the children of believers and pagan adults. Children were *always* considered under the umbrella of their parents' faith in the Bible, until they either embraced it themselves or rejected it, at which point they would receive either the blessings or the curses of the covenant. If God denies the sign and seal to infants of believers, it is because He denies them the grace signified by it. That means that all children of believers who die in their infancy *must be* hopelessly lost because God does not want them baptized. Ergo, He does not want them to have salvation. But that is not what the Bible teaches us. The Bible teaches us that children are proper subjects of Christ's kingdom (Matt. 18:6; 19:13-15; 21:16; Luke 10:21; 18:15-17). First Corinthians 7:14 only makes sense when considered under the covenantal view. I pray that believers would study this debated subject with joy in their hearts, seeking to know the truth so that they may happily conform their lives to it. "As for me and my house, we will serve the Lord."

Riddle me this... Despite all the facts we have just examined, if infant baptism is wrong and unbiblical, why are *so many* Baptists who are studying the subject *honestly* with open hearts converting and teaching, practicing, and defending it? Many who have adamantly written arguments against it have since refuted all their previous works and shown where their works were in error. Why is that? Let me say this... God rewards those who diligently seek Him and reveals His truths to those who earnestly and honestly want to know them.

Observe some of the historical records:

WESTMINSTER CONFESSION OF FAITH
Of the Sacraments. (Chapter 27)
I. Sacraments are holy signs and seals of the covenant of grace, immediately instituted by God, to represent Christ, and his benefits; and to confirm our interest in him: as also, to put a visible difference between those that belong unto the church, and the rest of the world; and solemnly to engage them to the service of Christ, according to his Word. (chap. 27)

Of Baptism. (Chapter 28)
I. Baptism is a sacrament of the new testament, ordained by Jesus Christ, not only for the solemn admission of the party baptized into the visible church; but also, to be unto him a sign and seal of the covenant of grace, of his ingrafting into Christ, of regeneration, of remission of sins, and of his giving up unto God, through Jesus Christ, to walk in newness of life. Which sacrament is, by God's own appointment, to be continued in his church until the end of the world. . . .

III. The grace which is exhibited in or by the sacraments rightly used, is not conferred by any power in them; neither doth the efficacy of a sacrament depend upon the piety or intention of him that doth administer it: but upon the work of the Spirit, and the word of institution, which contains, together with a precept authorizing the use thereof, a promise of benefit to worthy receivers.

IV. Not only those that do actually profess faith in and obedience unto Christ, but also the infants of one, or both, believing parents, are to be baptized. . . .

VI. The efficacy of Baptism is not tied to that moment of time wherein it is administered; yet, notwithstanding, by the right use of this ordinance, the grace promised is not only offered, but really exhibited, and conferred, by the Holy Ghost, to such (whether of age or infants) as that grace belongs unto, according to the counsel of God's own will, in his appointed time.

BELGIC CONFESSION, ARTICLE 34

...For that reason we detest the error of the Anabaptists, who are not content with a single baptism once received and also condemn the baptism of the children of believers. We believe our children ought to be baptized and sealed with the sign of the covenant, as little children were circumcised in Israel on the basis of the same promises made to our children.

And truly, Christ has shed his blood no less for washing the little children of believers than he did for adults. Therefore, they ought to receive the sign and sacrament of what Christ has done for them, just as the Lord commanded in the law that by offering a lamb for them the sacrament of the suffering and death of Christ would be granted them shortly after their birth. This was the sacrament of Jesus Christ.[1]

Furthermore, baptism does for our children what circumcision did for the Jewish people. That is why Paul calls baptism the "circumcision of Christ" (Colossians 2:12).

[1] The allusion here is to Lev. 12:6. Cf. Luke 2:22-24.

HEIDELBERG CATECHISM, QUESTION 74
Q. Should infants, too, be baptized?

A. Yes. For they as well as adults belong to God's covenant and community (Genesis 17:7) and no less than adults are promised forgiveness of sins through Christ's blood (Matthew 19:14) and the Holy Spirit, who produces faith (Psalm 22:10; Isaiah 44:1-3; Luke 1:15; Acts 2:38-39; 16:31).

Therefore, they, too, ought to be incorporated into the Christian church by baptism, the sign of the covenant, and distinguished from the children of unbelievers (Acts 10:47; 1 Corinthians 7:14). This was done in the Old Testament by circumcision (Genesis 17:9-14), in whose place baptism was instituted in the New Testament (Colossians 2:11-13).

SECOND HELVETIC CONFESSION, CHAPTER 20

6. We condemn the Anabaptists, who deny that young infants, born of faithful parents, are to be baptized. For, according to the doctrine of the gospel, "for of such is the kingdom of God" (Luke 18:16), and they are written in the covenant of God (Acts 3:25). Why, then, should not the sign of the covenant of God be given to them? Why should they not be consecrated by holy baptism, who are God's peculiar people and are in the Church of God? We condemn also the Anabaptists in the rest of those peculiar opinions which they hold against the Word of God. We therefore are not Anabaptists, neither do we agree with them in any point that is theirs.

WESTMINSTER CONFESSION OF FAITH, CHAPTER 28

4. Not only those that do actually profess faith in and obedience unto Christ (Mark 16:15-16), but also the infants of one, or both, believing parents, are to be baptized (Genesis 17:7, 9; Galatians 3:9, 14; Colossians 2:11-12; Acts 2:38-39; Romans 4:11-12; 1 Corinthians 7:14; Matthew 28:19; Mark 10:13-16; Luke 18:15)....

6. The efficacy of baptism is not tied to that moment of time wherein it is administered John 3:5, 8); yet, notwithstanding, by the right use of this ordinance, the grace promised is not only offered, but really exhibited, and conferred, by the Holy Ghost, to such (whether of age or infants) as that grace belongs unto, according to the counsel of God's own will, in his appointed time (Galatians 3:27; Titus 3:5; Ephesians 5:25-26; Acts 2:38, 41).

WESTMINSTER LARGER CHATECHISM, QUESTION 166

Q. Unto whom is baptism to be administered?

A. Baptism is not to be administered to any that are out of the visible church, and so strangers from the covenant of promise, till they profess their faith in Christ, and obedience to Him (Acts 8:36-38), but infants descending from parents, either both, or but one of them, professing faith in Christ, and obedience to Him, are in that respect within the covenant, and to be baptized (Genesis 17:7, 9; Galatians 3:9, 14; Colossians 2:11-12; Acts 2:38-39; Romans 4:11-12; 1 Corinthians 7:14; Matthew 28:19; Mark 10:13-16; Luke 18:15; Romans 11:16).

Baptism

14

BAPTISM AND MAKING DISCIPLES

"All authority has been given to Me in heaven and on earth. Go therefore and make disciples of all the nations, baptizing them in the name of the Father and the Son and the Holy Spirit, teaching them to observe all that I commanded you; and lo, I am with you always, even to the end of the age." **Matthew 28:18-20**

As James Montgomery Boice writes in his *Foundations of the Christian Faith*, "It is evident from those verses that baptism is an *initiatory* sacrament belonging to the task of *making disciples*."[8] [Emphasis mine.] What do you suppose the task of Christian parents is with regard to their children? Obviously it is making disciples.

John P. Sartelle wrote:

---

[8] Boice, *Foundations of the Christian Faith*, 597.

"It may seem that all you need to do is have your child baptized, and all will be well. That is what many modern church members think. They bring their children and have them baptized as if it were the ultimate fire insurance. But from that moment on you can see no difference between their home and the atheist family next door.

If you and your wife don't love each other as the Bible commands, if you don't teach your children Scripture, if you don't discipline them as God's Word teaches, if you don't pray with and for them daily, if Christ is not the center of your home, then you may baptize your children, but they will grow up just like children from non-Christian homes."[9]

Bryan Chapell wrote:

"We must confess that some bring their children for this sacrament because of the sweetness of the ceremony, or because of the traditions of family and church, or even with the misguided expectation that somehow 'holy water' will magically protect their child from hell. Yet neither sentiment nor tradition nor superstition is sufficient reason for believers to bring their children to be baptized. And, thankfully, such reasons are not the basis of our church's practice. We baptize infants because we believe that the Bible teaches us to do so."[10]

God said this about Abraham:

"For I have chosen him in order that he may command his children and his household after him to

---

[9] John P. Sartelle, *What Christian Parents Should Know About Infant Baptism*, (Phillipsburg, NJ: P&R Publishing, 1985), 19.
[10] Chapell, *Why Do We Baptize Infants?*, 1.

keep the way of the Lord." **Genesis 18:19**

It was Abraham's responsibility to teach his child about God in every facet of his home. Circumcision was not insurance that God would automatically save Isaac. It was the sign of a covenant that he would raise his son in the Lord and that God would have regard for him. It is the same with baptism. Baptism is not insurance that God will automatically save your children. It is the sign of a covenant that you will raise your children in the Lord and that God will have regard for them. Here is just some of what Scripture has to say on the subject of Christian parents making disciples out of their children:

> "And you shall teach [these words, which I am commanding you today,] diligently to your sons and shall talk of them when you sit in your house and when you walk by the way and when you lie down and when you rise up." **Deuteronomy 6:7**

> "And you shall teach [these words of mine] to your sons, talking of them when you sit in your house and when you walk along the road and when you lie down and when you rise up." **Deuteronomy 11:19**

> "Train up a child in the way he should go: and when he is old, he will not depart from it." **Proverbs 22:6**

Parents who bring their children to be baptized are presented with this vow:

> Do you now unreservedly dedicate your children to God, and promise, in humble reliance upon divine grace, that you will endeavour to set before him/her a godly example, that you will pray with and for him/her, that you will teach him/her the doctrines of

our holy faith, and that you will strive, by all the means of God's appointment, to bring him/her up in the nurture and admonition of the Lord?[11]

If these parents are bringing a second, third, fourth, etc., child to be baptized, they should be asked this question in addition to the vow:

Have you so kept the vow you made before God with your previous child that you can take this vow with a sincere and clear conscience?[12]

Mr. Sartelle warns parents against making vows they do not intend to follow through on (much like wedding vows to many couples these days) and that do not mean a thing to them: "Parents, don't make a vow to the Lord just as a social nicety. Imagine, coming before the living God and mouthing words that mean nothing to you just to gain social respectability! If you do that, the blood of your children will be upon your own head. It shall be written of you in eternity that you trifled with the Almighty God."[13]

David C. Jones poses the following questions: "Are [these little ones, by virtue of their parents' relationship to Christ,] also brought into a new relationship with Christ even though they are too young intellectually to apprehend the gospel and to appropriate it for themselves in the conscious exercise of repentance and faith? Does their psychological inability to fulfill the conditions required of adult converts render the idea of discipleship meaningless so far as infants and small children are concerned? Or, [is their covenant status to be granted and baptism to be administered to them, and] are they to be discipled along with their believing parents, given the solidarity of the family unit?" His question about

[11] Sartelle, *What Christian Parents Should Know About Infant Baptism*, 20.
[12] Ibid.
[13] Ibid, 21.

psychological inability is something we need to consider deeply. What about mentally handicapped persons, who, even in adulthood, have the psychological inability to fulfill the conditions required of adult converts? Does this mean there is no hope for the mentally handicapped? "Go therefore and make disciples of all the nations, baptizing them in the name of the Father and the Son and the Holy Spirit, teaching them to observe all that I commanded you" (Matt. 28:19-20).